Please do not remove

Transaction Card

Steal Away

AFRICA EXULTING, ECHOES IN RESPONSIVE ACCLAMATION, WILBERFORCE! AND THE FETTERED SLAVE SHAKES HIS CHAINS WITH JOY. *

Steal Away

SLAVES TELL THEIR OWN STORIES

EDITED WITH AN INTRODUCTION BY
Abraham Chapman

ERNEST BENN LIMITED · LONDON

First published 1971 by Praeger Publishers Inc.
111 Fourth Avenue, New York, N.Y. 10003, U.S.A.

© Abraham Chapman 1971

This revised edition published 1973 by Ernest Benn Limited
25 New Street Square, London EC4A 3JA

© Abraham Chapman 1973

Printed in Great Britain

ISBN 0 510–10205–0

For my grandson, Daniel

CONTENTS

List of Illustrations   ix

Acknowledgements   xi

Introduction   xiii

Olaudah Equiano (Gustavas Vassa): "I Had Never
  Heard of White Men or Europeans, nor of the Sea"   1

Ottobah Cugoano: "I Was Early Snatched Away from
  My Native Country"   29

Belinda: "The Cruelty of Men, Whose Faces Were Like
  the Moon"   38

Ignatius Sancho: "A Tear in Favour of My Miserable
  Black Brethren" (A Letter to Laurence Sterne, author
  of *Tristram Shandy*)   44

Austin Steward: Slave Life on the Plantation   48

Thomas Jones: How I Learned to Read and Write   66

William Wells Brown: The Goopher King   76

Josiah Henson: Father Henson's Story   86

Elizabeth Keckley: The Sorrows of Girlhood   103

The Reverend Henry Highland Garnet: A Former Slave
  Appeals to the Slaves of the United States of America   115

Jourdon Anderson: Letter from a Freedman to His Old
  Master   127

Frederick Douglass: The Heroic Slave   131

Suggestions for Further Reading   182

LIST OF ILLUSTRATIONS

1   The capture of slaves in Africa   10

2   The captured slaves are marched in coffles to the
    coast   22

3   Weaker slaves were abandoned on the march and
    left to die   30

4   Lieutenant Henn's sketch of the slave market in
    Zanzibar   34

5   The loading plan of the slave ship *Brookes* (1839)   40/41

6   Slaves imported to be sold in the British West Indies   46

7   Revolt of slaves aboard the *Amistad* (1839)   56/57

8   A sale of slaves in the Rotunda, New Orleans   62

9   On the auction block   71

10 Beatings with specially designed instruments were
    used to subjugate the slaves   77

11 Elaborate systems for whipping slaves are exposed
    in the *American Anti-Slavery Almanac for 1838*   83

12 A page from the *American Anti-Slavery Almanac
    for 1838* attacks the denial of marital and family
    rights of slaves   89

13 The runaway slave was a heroic symbol for the
    abolitionists   92

14 Runaway slaves had to evade the "patrollers"
    constantly scouring the South   97

15 Poster advertising dogs trained to catch runaway
    slaves   108

16 Reaching the North was no guarantee of freedom
    for the runaway slave   117

17 Poster advertising a reward for the return of a
    runaway slave   129

18 Call to the Wisconsin State Anti-Slave-Catchers'
    convention   135

19 Poster in opposition to the harsher fugitive slave
    law of 1850   150

20 The smuggling of runaways into Boston at night   170

ACKNOWLEDGEMENTS

The author and publishers wish to record their grateful thanks to copyright owners for the use of the illustrations listed below:

The Mansell Collection for: frontispiece, 1, 2, 3, 4, 6, 8, 9, 14

The Schomburg Collection, New York Public Library for: 5

The Special Slavery Collection, Rare Book Department, Cornell University Library for: 15

The State Historical Society of Wisconsin for: 7, 10, 11, 12, 13, 16, 17, 18, 19, 20

INTRODUCTION

In this book I have brought together selections from the very rich, long-neglected, and largely forgotten body of literature known as the slave narratives. This special category of narratives in the English language emerged and developed when slavery flourished in the British colonies in America and in the United States. It consists of stories told by the slaves who succeeded in running away from their "owners" to free territory in the Northern states of the U.S.A., Canada, or England. These stories, for the first time, expressed the slave's view of slavery and became a very important current of anti-slavery literature in the United States and Britain. Quite a few of the slave narratives were originally published in England.

Many of these stories were literally "told", dictated by runaways who could not write, because in the slave states it was a crime "to teach, or attempt to teach, any slave . . . to read or write" or "sell to such slave or slaves any books or pamphlets" because "the teaching of slaves to read and write, has a tendency to excite dissatisfaction in their minds, and to produce insurrection and rebellion." Thus declared the law of the State of North Carolina, which was typical of the slave code statutes of the South.

According to the masters' plan, the slaves were to be denied the possibilities of self-expression and the ability to tell the truth about slavery and their lives and aspirations. They had to give up their native African languages in a new and hostile land, and they were forbidden education in English. But no force on earth could stifle the voice of the slaves. They took the words and languages of their conquerors and transformed them into their own vocabularies. Whenever possible, slaves secretly defied the laws and mastered the tools of literacy while still in slavery (as the story of Thomas Jones in this book shows) and others learned to read and write after escaping to areas where they could teach themselves or could get to school. All but two of the stories in this book were written by their authors. The exceptions are "Father Henson's Story" (which was originally dictated by Josiah Henson to "an editorial helper" and in a later edition revised by Henson himself), and the petition of Belinda to the legislature of Massachusetts.

The slaves created a rich oral literature in their new tongue and a distinct culture to sustain themselves intellectually and spiritually and to give expression to the *man* in the slave in opposition to the dehumanizing conditions of slavery. The title of this book is taken from the words of one of the popular old slave songs or spirituals:

> Steal away, steal away, steal away to Jesus,
> Steal away, steal away home,
> I ain't got long to stay here.

Slaves could gather together only for religious worship, and beyond the expression of strictly controlled, permissible religious sentiments, the spirituals provided the imagery and a veiled structure for the utterance of hidden, uncontrollable freedom aspirations. "Jesus" and "home" symbolize here liberty from bondage and a haven from the harsh inhumanity of slave life. The strange idiom "steal away" carried the meaning of secret escape and can best be understood if it is recalled that in the eighteenth and nineteenth centuries the anti-slavery forces spoke of slavery as "manstealing."

Frederick Douglass, the great Black abolitionist leader, writer, and statesman, wrote:

> The more I read, the more I was led to abhor and detest my enslavers. I could regard them in no other light than a band of successful robbers, who had left their homes, and gone to Africa, and stolen us from our homes, and in a strange land reduced us to slavery.

One of the most famous anti-slavery pronouncements in Puritan America, a sermon in 1791 by Reverend Jonathan Edwards, the well-known son of an even more famous Puritan father, referred to the slave traders as "licensed robbers." In this sermon, which was reprinted in pamphlet and other forms countless times in the course of the struggle against slavery, he argued:

> But to steal a man or to rob him of his liberty is a greater sin, than to steal his property, or take it by violence. And to hold a man in a state of slavery, who has a right to his liberty, is to be every day guilty of robbing him of his liberty, or of manstealing . . . You will not deny that liberty is more valuable than property; and that it is a greater sin to deprive a man of his whole liberty during life, than to deprive him of his whole property; or that manstealing is a greater crime than robbery. Nor will you deny, that to hold in slavery a man who was stolen, is substantially the same crime as to steal him . . . This question seems to be clearly decided by revelation (Exod. xxi. 16): "He that stealeth a man and selleth him, or if he be found in his hand, he shall surely be put to death." Thus death is, by the divine express declaration, the punishment due to the crime of manstealing.

The legal status of slaves was that of property, but unlike other stolen property slaves refused to remain stolen. Slaves stole away from their stealers and all of the stories in this book are by slaves who had "stolen away" or were able to devise ways of buying their freedom from their owners. They are presented because of their interest as stories and as literature, but they are important as history as well.

Here and there some of the language of the narratives may strike the modern reader as old-fashioned, but they are the authentic sounds and forms of expression of the not-too-distant past. To understand the paradoxes, contradictions, racial conflicts, and wars of the modern world, it is important to remember and examine the past and particularly the part that slavery played in the development of the modern world.

In the strange and terrible ways of the movement of history, slavery was one of the foundations on which modern, industrial, Western societies and economies were built.

The origins of slavery stretch back to antiquity. The narratives in this book illuminate *modern slavery*, developed by the strongest countries of Europe, which penetrated Africa, evolved the vast African slave trade, and employed slave labor in developing plantations and other economic enterprises in the Americas. The actual number of Africans torn away from Africa in the slave trade is not known, but estimates are as high as 20 or 30 million. It has been designated the greatest migration in human history and it was an involuntary one.

The commercial expansion of Europe, the accumulation of capital for the development of modern capitalism, the development of modern shipping and maritime power, depended heavily on the slave trade. These compelling economic advantages overpowered the cries of protest against its inhumanity, and modern slavery could emerge as an international system and important economic institution of the modern industrial era and the Age of the Enlightenment, when ideological homage to the doctrines of democracy was at a peak. Slavery was the most glaring revelation of the disparity between the promises and hopes of democracy and the severe limitations of its performance for large segments of society and humanity.

The overwhelming majority of the African slaves were transported across the Atlantic. More than 2 million were brought to the British West Indies, a major slave center, and from there were further distributed throughout the Caribbean and the Southern states of the U.S.A. Many millions more were transported to Brazil.

Britain's involvement with slavery was primarily with the slave trade. No plantation system depending upon slave labor evolved in Britain. The actual number of African slaves in England did not exceed 15,000. Slaves were frequently used as servants by the wealthy and as symbols of affluence by their owners. A poem by Charles Dunster depicting London high society as it paraded St. James's Street gives us this picture:

> . . . Sometimes at their head,
> Index of Rank or Opulence supreme,
> A sable Youth from Aethiopia's climes,
> In milk-white turban dight, precedes the Train.

But slavery was nevertheless a very important source of wealth for Britain. In the rivalry between the maritime powers, she secured the commanding position in the European slave trade and British companies and ships transported millions of slaves across the Atlantic. Bristol was the first major British slave-trading port, but, after 1750, Liverpool became the greatest port of slave ships in all of Europe. Memories and relics of the slave trade are a part of the heritage of Liverpool, still alive today. John Lennon, of the Beatles, spoke of this in a recent interview in New York. "The slaves were brought to Liverpool and then to America. On the riverfront in Liverpool you can see the rings inside where they were chained up."

The echoes of history in Lennon's mind are very real, but one of his historical impressions is not entirely accurate. The slave ships arriving in Liverpool did not bring very many of the slaves taken out of Africa into England. The slave trade was a triangular one. The ships would leave Liverpool with cloth and supplies for the trade for slaves on the West coast of Africa. African slaves would then be carried across the Atlantic to the slave markets in the West Indies. There the ships would take on rum, sugar, and tobacco and carry them back to Liverpool.

Slaves in England, as in the United States and wherever they were held in bondage, would run away when they could. The following advertisement, for example, appeared in a London newspaper in 1711:

On Monday last, a Negroe Boy, about 14 Years old, of a good Complexion, indifferent Tall, speaks good English, with a Drugget Coat, Silk Waistcoat, with Red and Yellow Stripes, run away . . .

In the eighteenth century there were numerous Negro beggars in London. Many of them were cast-off slaves, and they were then called "St. Giles blackbirds." Negroes appear in many of Hogarth's engravings depicting London life of his time.

In England itself, slavery did not have the support of any statute law and the courts ruled on its legality in various ways. In 1705, Chief Justice Holt declared: "As soon as a Negro comes into England he becomes free." In 1729, however, the King's attorney and solicitor general denied this. But in 1773, in the famous case of the runaway slave James Somerset, who escaped while in England, Lord Mansfield finally settled the legal issue. He declared that slavery was "so odious that nothing can be suffered to support it, but positive law" and in the absence of any such law in England he ruled that "the Black must be discharged."

This decision did not diminish Britain's leadership in the continuing slave trade and Parliament did not act to halt slavery in the British colonies until quite some time after the American War of Independence. The anti-slavery movement in England, which began in the 1720s, ultimately concentrated on efforts to abolish the slave trade. In 1787, Thomas Clarkson, William Wilberforce, and other British abolitionists organized the Society for Effecting the Abolition of the Slave Trade. In 1807, the British slave trade was brought to a close, and in 1833 Parliament enacted a bill for the abolition of slavery in the remaining British colonies.

In America, the former British colonies in the North of the United States began to outlaw slavery immediately after the War of Independence. The constitution of the state of Vermont, in 1777, was the first to abolish slavery. By 1784, slavery had been abolished in Massachusetts, Connecticut, and Rhode Island, and manumission acts were passed in New York in

1785, and in New Jersey in 1786. In the Southern states slavery remained legal until the Emancipation Proclamation in 1863 and the ratification of the Thirteenth Amendment to the Constitution of the United States in 1865.

The outlawing of slavery in the northern states did not turn the North into a haven for slaves who escaped from the South. The first fugitive slave law was enacted in 1793. It empowered the slave-owners to seize interstate fugitives wherever found, to bring them before any federal or state magistrate in the vicinity, and to obtain a certificate warranting their removal to the state from which they had escaped. This law did not provide trial by jury, and it authorized conviction solely on the oral testimony of the claimant or on an affidavit certified by a magistrate of the slave state from which the fugitive was alleged to have escaped. It was not easy to enforce this law in the North, but it was a federal law of the United States that gave aid and support to the slave-owners of the South and to the institution of slavery. In 1850, a harsher and more stringent fugitive slave act was passed, and hunts for fugitive slaves in the North were intensified.

No laws could prevent slaves from trying to escape to freedom and in all the years that slavery was legal the movement of runaway slaves and the "Underground Railroad" never abated. In the voluminous literature about slavery in America, the full size and scope of the movement of runaway slaves still remains largely unexplored.

Official Southern authorities and defenders of slavery cultivated the myth of the happy and contented slave, but in their more candid moments they addressed themselves to the very practical problem of immense property losses to the South because of an uncontrollable and steady stream of runaway slaves. One Southern writer, J. F. H. Claiborne, complained that the second Fugitive Slave Law had failed to make "provision for the restitution to the South of $30,000,000, of which she had been plundered through the 100,000 slaves abducted from her in the course of the last forty years"—that is, from 1810 to 1850.

Slaves began to run away from their owners long before 1810. And in the decade and more between 1850 and the Civil War the stream of runaways continued uninterruptedly or with even mounted momentum. If we base an estimate on this Southern pro-slavery source, it would appear that the number of slaves who escaped to the North was well beyond 100,000, how much beyond we have no accurate way of knowing. Uncounted, too, are the numbers of slaves who escaped south of the border, to Mexico, from Louisiana and Texas and the southernmost slave states.

To appreciate the full magnitude of the runaway movement we must also bear in mind the many, many thousands of slaves who embarked upon the road to freedom but never reached their goal because they were caught by the highly organized network of patrollers, bloodhounds, slave-hunters, and spies, elaborately designed to prevent escapes. The famous Anti-Slavery Tract on *The Fugitive Slave Law and Its Victims*, published in 1861, speaks of "that company of slaves" who "are overtaken before reaching the Free States."

What was the ratio of those who reached liberty to those who tried to escape? With all the hazards and traps of the manhunts for runaways, is it reasonable to suppose that more slaves were caught searching for freedom than the number of those who actually escaped the South? The deeper you get into the realities depicted in the slave narratives the more insistently this question haunts you. Is it possible that the escape movement involved perhaps hundreds of thousands of slaves? Nobody knows. The more slave narratives I read the more references I found to runaway slaves who were caught before they succeeded in making their escape, caught and returned to slavery. And many references, too, to runaways who were caught and ran away again, repeatedly, notwithstanding the punishments they had to suffer after they were captured.

In one of the autobiographical slave narratives that space does not permit me to use in this collection, *From Log Cabin to the Pulpit, Or, Fifteen Years in Slavery* by Reverend W. H. Robinson, a book of reminiscences of the author's early life in slavery published in 1913, we read:

> I knew my only hope of escape was to run away, so I started at once. I had often heard ex-runaway slaves, men and women, tell the adventures of when they were in the woods and about their hiding places or rendezvous. I had heard it told so often at my father's fireside that I knew almost directly where they were, for I had passed close by them many times, so I started to look for them.

He goes on to tell how he found a rocky mound or cave, near a pond, after wading through the water, and there he discovered a whole group of runaways, eighteen in number, who had been living there as a group, hunting for food, standing guard, and dividing their duties to sustain the group. Some had been hiding out for as long as eleven months. He became the nineteenth member of the band, but finally they were all captured, severely punished, and forced back into slave labor. In the narratives in this collection you will find other references to escaping slaves who were caught before they could reach the end of the road.

The routes of escape were numerous, ingenious, dangerous, and complex. They were graphically summarized by William Still, the great Afro-American leader of the Philadelphia Branch of the "Underground Railroad," in his Preface to his voluminous book *The Underground Railroad*, first published in 1872, based upon his long years of work with, and for, the runaway slaves. He wrote:

> In these Records will be found interesting narratives of the escapes of many men, women and children, from the prison-house of bondage; from cities and plantations; from rice swamps and

cotton fields; from kitchens and mechanic shops; from Border States and Gulf States; from cruel masters and mild masters;— some guided by the north star alone, penniless, braving the perils of land and sea; eluding the keen scent of the bloodhound as well as the more dangerous pursuit of the savage slave-hunter; some from secluded dens and caves of the earth, where for months and years they had been hidden away waiting for the chance to escape; from mountains and swamps, where indescribable suffering from hunger and other privations had patiently been endured. Occasionally fugitives came in boxes and chests, and not infrequently some were secreted in steamers and vessels, and in some instances journeyed hundreds of miles in skiffs. Men disguised in female attire and women dressed in the garb of men have under very trying circumstances triumphed in thus making their way to freedom. And here and there when all other modes of escape seemed cut off, some, whose fair complexions have rendered them indistinguishable from their Anglo-Saxon brethren, feeling that they could endure the yoke no longer, with assumed airs of importance, such as they had been accustomed to see their masters show when traveling, have taken the usual modes of conveyance and have even braved the most scrutinizing inspection of slave-holders, slave-catchers and car conductors, who were ever on the alert to catch those who were considered base and white enough to practice such deception. Passes have been written and used by fugitives, with their masters' and mistresses' names boldly attached thereto, and have answered admirably as a protection, when passing through ignorant country districts of slave regions, where but few, either white or colored, knew how to read or write correctly.

That there were slaves who were crushed and maimed and beaten into submission by the chains and whips and brutalities of slavery is hardly a surprise. The wonder is that so many thousands and thousands of slaves refused to submit, escaped or died trying to escape.

In the face of all this, to continue to stress submissiveness as the predominant characteristic of the slaves in the United States and to raise the figure of a servile "Sambo" as the symbol of the slave personality, as some contemporary historians do, is to ignore the significant evidence of the slave narratives.

Now that many of the slave narratives which have been inaccessible for so long are being reprinted in various modern editions, all students of slavery, Black history, and the human personality can turn to them and discover for themselves the light they have to shed on these very important questions.

The slave narratives created a new image in American literature: *the slave as hero.* And some of the reactions to the publication of the slave narratives reflect the first conscious awareness of this new type of hero in American literature.

One of the early slave narratives published in the United States, *A Narrative of the Life and Adventures of Venture, A Native of Africa: But Resident Above Sixty Years in the United States of America, Related by Himself,* published in New London, Connecticut in 1798, opened with an anonymous Preface, most probably by the person to whom Venture Smith related his story. It noted:

> The reader is here presented with an account, not of a renowned politician or warrior, but of an untutored African slave, brought into this Christian country at eight years of age, wholly destitute of all education but what he received in common with other domesticated animals, enjoying no advantages that could lead him to suppose himself superior to the beasts, his fellow servants . . . The reader may see a Franklin and a Washington, in a state of nature, or rather in a state of slavery. Destitute as he is of all education, and broken by hardships and infirmities of age, he still exhibits striking traces of native ingenuity and good sense.

Patronizing as the tone of the preface as a whole is, it reflects the beginnings of a new consciousness which the slave narratives were creating as far back as the eighteenth century: a sense of the heroic in the slave evident in the reference to the national heroes Benjamin Franklin and George Washington shortly after the American Revolution.

In November, 1849, the Unitarian magazine *The Christian Examiner and Religious Miscellany* published a lengthy 32 page article entitled "Narratives of Fugitive Slaves," devoted to a review in depth of five books which had been published in 1848 and 1849: the narratives of Henry Watson, Lewis and Milton Clarke, William W. Brown, Frederick Douglass, and Josiah Henson. This article declared:

> America has the mournful honor of adding a new department to the literature of civilization,—the autobiographies of escaped slaves. We have placed below the titles of five narratives of this description . . . We place these volumes without hesitation among the most remarkable productions of the age,—remarkable as being pictures of slavery by the slave, remarkable as disclosing under a new light the mixed elements of American civilization, and not less remarkable as a vivid exhibition of the force and working of the native love of freedom in the individual mind . . . There is that in the lives of men who have sufficient force of mind and heart to enable them to struggle up from hopeless bondage to the position of freemen, beside which the ordinary characters of romance are dull and tame. They encounter a whole Iliad of woes, not in plundering and enslaving others, but in recovering for themselves those rights of which they have been deprived from birth. Or if the Iliad should be thought not to present a parallel case, we know not where one who wished to write a modern Odyssey could find a better subject than in the adventures of a fugitive slave. What a combination of qualities and deeds and sufferings most fitted to attract human sympathy in each particular case!

The same issue of *Putnam's Monthly* that published one of the serial installments of *Benito Cereno*, Herman Melville's novella dealing with a slave uprising aboard a slave ship (November, 1855), also published a review of *My Bondage and My Freedom* by Frederick Douglass extolling his genius.

Another significant point is made in a narrative published in 1859, *The Rev. J. W. Loguen, As A Slave And As A Freeman: A Narrative Of Real Life*. Although this narrative assumed the form of a third-person biography, it is quite commonly accepted that it was actually an autobiographical narrative written by Reverend Loguen himself, a former slave. In the Preface we read:

> For a long time invisible mental powers have been turning society on its hinges to let in a new dispensation of learning, religion, and life. There is a spring in all departments of humanity for a "long pull, a strong pull, all-together," to move mankind on to a higher and a better level; and our young readers should know that colored men furnish a quota of the mental and physical muscle that produces the motion. Society is in process of incubation, and we should know whence is the heat and substance that embody and cherish the embryo. We should keep an eye on the formative elements, to see what portion is subsiding and dying, and what portion is combining to form the substance and life of the coming age. The African element contributes largely to the causes that agitate mankind, and must have its place in the product. The vital powers are attracted to it by force of the charities that make them vital, and are amalgamating with that element to form a new basis of heaven, humanity, and religion—when men may look at it, and not start back affrighted . . . At such a time, colored men are Divine instrumentalities for Divine ends. Hence, so many of them have dodged their masters and their chains,— broken through the clouds, and become conspicuous in the intellectual and moral firmament.

This new and important current of literature revealed images and truths that challenged the prevailing racist stereotypes in American thought and literature depicting "the slave" as passive, submissive, lazy, lacking in ingenuity, and stupid. The slave narratives had a marked influence on the whole development of the anti-slavery novel in American fiction. The strange thing is that in the twentieth century all but a few of the most famous slave narratives were largely forgotten and ignored, out of sight and out of mind. Historians can have very poor memories as is evident in a scholarly article in *The Louisiana*

Historical Quarterly (January 1939) which could say: "What was it like to be a slave? We do not know. The slaves themselves have never told."

And to this day prominent writers, attempting to recreate in historical fiction the lives and personalities of slaves, can still indicate in their public statements very limited recognition of the rich body of slave narratives which are an indispensable source of the thinking and feelings of former slaves.

We are now witnessing, at long last, a revival of interest in the slave narratives and many of the full texts of long-out-of-print narratives are now being reprinted in the United States. This is a welcome development.

In this book I present selections from a variety of different types of slave narratives, for their story and narrative interest and value. I have included the complete text of the novella *The Heroic Slave* by Frederick Douglass, which actually marks the beginnings of significant Afro-American fiction in the United States, reprinted in full for the first time since its initial appearance in 1853.

This book is not an exact reprint of the American edition published in New York in 1971. Some of the narratives in the American edition have been replaced by other narratives in this edition, and this introduction and the editor's notes introducing the individual narratives have been written especially for this British edition.

Abraham Chapman

OLAUDAH EQUIANO
(GUSTAVAS VASSA)

Memories of life in Africa and the shocks of kidnap, captivity, and the slave ships are vivid in the early slave narratives. *The Interesting Narrative of the Life of Olaudah Equiano, or Gustavas Vassa, The African*, first published in London in 1789, was the bestseller of the eighteenth-century slave narratives and has been republished time and again in numerous editions. The author's two names illustrate one of the many ways the slave-owners used to try and destroy the African personality: refusal to recognize the African names. Equiano was sold into slavery in Virginia, was called Michael by his first owner, Jacob by others, and was finally named Gustavus Vassa by a lieutenant in the British Royal Navy who purchased him "for a present for some of his friends in England." By that time he had learned to speak English and he recalls that when given his new name "I refused to be called so, and told them as well as I could that I would be called Jacob; but he said I should not, and still called me Gustav; and when I refused to answer to my new name, which at first I did, it gained me many a cuff; so at length I submitted and was obliged to bear the present name, by which I have been known ever since."

He was more fortunate than most slaves in that he was able to become literate and ultimately to purchase his freedom from his last master. He settled in England and participated actively in the anti-slavery movement. He prefaced the publication of his narrative with an open letter to the members of Parliament in which he said:

Permit me, with the greatest deference and respect, to lay at your feet the following genuine narrative; the chief design of which is to excite in your august assemblies a sense of compassion for the miseries which the Slave-Trade has entailed on my unfortunate countrymen. By the horrors of that trade was I first torn away from all the tender connections that were naturally dear to my heart . . . I am sensible I ought to entreat your pardon for addressing to you a work so wholly devoid of literary merit; but, as the production of an unlettered African, who is actuated by the hope of becoming an instrument towards the relief of his suffering countrymen, I trust that such a man, pleading in such a cause, will be acquitted of boldness and presumption.

Following are the first two chapters, slightly abridged, of the fourteen chapters of his narrative.

"I Had Never Heard of White Men or Europeans, nor of the Sea"

CHAPTER 1

That part of Africa, known by the name of Guinea, to which the trade for slaves is carried on, extends along the coast above 3400 miles, from Senegal to Angola, and includes a variety of kingdoms. Of these the most considerable is the kingdom of Benin, both as to extent and wealth, the richness and cultivation of the soil, the power of its king, and the number and warlike disposition of the inhabitants. It is situated nearly under the line, and extends along the coast about 170 miles, but runs back into the interior part of Africa to a distance hitherto, I believe, unexplored by any traveller, and seems only terminated at length by the empire of Abyssinia, near 1500 miles from its beginning. This kingdom is divided into many provinces or districts, in one of the most remote and fertile of which, I was born, in the year 1745, situated in a charming fruitful vale, named Essaka. The distance of this province from the capital of Benin and the sea coast must be very considerable, for I had never heard of white men or Europeans, nor of the sea; and our subjection to the king of Benin was little more than nominal, for every transaction of the government, as far as my slender observation extended, was conducted by the chief or elders of the place. The manners and government of a people who have little commerce with other countries are generally very simple, and the history of what passes in one family or village may serve as a specimen of the whole nation. My father was one of those elders or chiefs I have spoken of, and was styled Embrenche, a term, as I remember, importing the highest distinction, and signifying in our language a *mark* of grandeur. This mark is conferred on the person entitled to it, by cutting the skin across the top of the forehead, and drawing it down to the eyebrows; and while it is in this situation applying a warm hand, and rubbing it until it shrinks up into a thick *weal* across the lower part of the forehead. Most of the judges and senators were thus marked; my father had long borne it; I had seen it conferred on one of my brothers, and I also was *destined* to receive it by my parents. Those Embrenche, or chief men, decided disputes and punished crimes, for which purpose they always assembled together. The proceedings were generally short, and in most cases the law of retaliation prevailed. I remember a man was brought before my father, and the other judges, for kidnapping a boy; and, although he was the son of a chief or senator, he was condemned to make recompense by a man or woman slave. Adultery, however, was sometimes punished with slavery or death, a punishment which I believe is inflicted on it throughout most of the nations of Africa,* so sacred among them is the honor of the marriage bed, and so jealous are they of the fidelity of their

* See Benezet's "Account of Guinea," throughout.

wives. Of this I recollect an instance—a woman was convicted before the judges of adultery, and delivered over, as the custom was, to her husband, to be punished. Accordingly he determined to put her to death; but it being found, just before her execution, that she had an infant at her breast, and no woman being prevailed on to perform the part of a nurse, she was spared on account of the child. The men, however, do not preserve the same constancy to their wives which they expect from them; for they indulge in a plurality, though seldom in more than two. Their mode of marriage is thus—both parties are usually betrothed when young by their parents (though I have known the males to betroth themselves). On this occasion a feast is prepared, and the bride and bridegroom stand up in the midst of all their friends, who are assembled for the purpose, while he declares she is henceforth to be looked upon as his wife, and that no other person is to pay any addresses to her. This is also immediately proclaimed in the vicinity, on which the bride retires from the assembly. Some time after, she is brought home to her husband, and then another feast is made, to which the relations of both parties are invited; her parents then deliver her to the bridegroom, accompanied with a number of blessings, and at the same time they tie around her waist a cotton string of the thickness of a goosequill, which none but married women are permitted to wear; she is now considered as completely his wife; and at this time the dowry is given to the new married pair, which generally consists of portions of land, slaves, and cattle, household goods, and implements of husbandry. These are offered by the friends of both parties; besides which the parents of the bridegroom present gifts to those of the bride, whose property she is looked upon before marriage; but after it she is esteemed the sole property of her husband. The ceremony being now ended, the festival begins, which is celebrated with bonfires and loud acclamations of joy, accompanied with music and dancing.

We are almost a nation of dancers, musicians, and poets. Thus every great event, such as a triumphant return from battle or other cause of public rejoicing, is celebrated in public dances, which are accompanied with songs and music suited to the occasion. The assembly is separated into four divisions, which dance either apart or in succession, and each with a character peculiar to itself. The first division contains the married men, who in their dances frequently exhibit feats of arms and the representation of a battle. To these succeed the married women, who dance in the second division. The young men occupy the third, and the maidens the fourth. Each represents some interesting scene of real life, such as a great achievement, domestic employment, a pathetic story, or some rural sport; and as the subject is generally founded on some recent event, it is therefore ever new. This gives our dances a spirit and variety which I have scarcely seen elsewhere.* We have many musical instruments, particularly drums of different kinds, a piece of music which resembles a guitar, and another much like a stickado. These last are chiefly used by betrothed virgins, who play on them on all grand festivals.

As our manners are simple, our luxuries are few. The dress of both sexes is nearly the same. It generally consists of a long piece of calico, or muslin, wrapped loosely round the body, somewhat in the form of a highland plaid. This is usually dyed blue, which is our favorite color. It is extracted from a berry, and is brighter and richer than any I have seen in Europe. Besides this, our women of distinction wear golden ornaments, which they dispose with some profusion on their arms and legs. When our women are not employed with the men in tillage, their usual occupation is spinning and weaving cotton, which they afterwards dye, and make into garments. They also manufacture earthen vessels, of which we have many kinds. Among the rest, tobacco pipes, made after the

---

* When I was in Smyrna I have frequently seen the Greeks dance after this manner.

same fashion, and used in the same manner, as those in Turkey.*

Our manner of living is entirely plain; for as yet the natives are unacquainted with those refinements in cookery which debauch the taste; bullocks, goats, and poultry supply the greatest part of their food. (These constitute likewise the principal wealth of the country, and the chief articles of its commerce.) The flesh is usually stewed in a pan; to make it savory we sometimes use pepper, and other spices, and we have salt made of wood ashes. Our vegetables are mostly plantains, eadas, yams, beans, and Indian corn. The head of the family usually eats alone; his wives and slaves have also their separate tables. Before we taste food we always wash our hands; indeed, our cleanliness on all occasions is extreme, but on this it is an indispensable ceremony. After washing, libation is made, by pouring out a small portion of the drink on the floor, and tossing a small quantity of the food in a certain place, for the spirits of departed relations, which the natives suppose to preside over their conduct and guard them from evil. They are totally unacquainted with strong or spirituous liquors; and their principal beverage is palm wine. This is got from a tree of that name, by tapping it at the top and fastening a large gourd to it; and sometimes one tree will yield three or four gallons in a night. When just drawn it is of a most delicious sweetness; but in a few days it acquires a tartish and more spirituous flavor, though I never saw anyone intoxicated by it. The same tree also produces nuts and oil. Our principal luxury is in perfumes: one sort of these is an odoriferous wood of delicious fragrance, the other a kind of earth, a small portion of which thrown into the fire diffuses

---

* The bowl is earthen, curiously figured, to which a long reed is fixed as a tube. This tube is sometimes so long as to be borne by one, and frequently out of grandeur, two boys.

a most powerful odor.* We beat this wood into powder, and mix it with palm oil, with which both men and women perfume themselves.

In our buildings we study convenience rather than ornament. Each master of a family has a large square piece of ground, surrounded with a moat or fence, or enclosed with a wall made of red earth tempered, which, when dry, is as hard as brick. Within this, are his houses to accommodate his family and slaves, which, if numerous, frequently present the appearance of a village. In the middle, stands the principal building, appropriated to the sole use of the master and consisting of two apartments; in one of which he sits in the day with his family, the other is left apart for the reception of his friends. He has besides these a distinct apartment in which he sleeps, together with his male children. On each side are the apartments of his wives, who have also their separate day and night houses. The habitations of the slaves and their families are distributed throughout the rest of the enclosure. These houses never exceed one story in height; they are always built of wood, or stakes driven into the ground, crossed with wattles, and neatly plastered within and without. The roof is thatched with reeds. Our day houses are left open at the sides; but those in which we sleep are always covered, and plastered in the inside, with a composition mixed with cow-dung, to keep off the different insects, which annoy us during the night. The walls and floors also of these are generally covered with mats. Our beds consist of a platform, raised three or four feet from the ground, on which are laid skins, and different parts of a spongy tree, called plantain. Our covering is calico or muslin, the same as our dress. The usual seats are a few logs of wood; but we have benches, which are generally perfumed to accommodate strangers:

* When I was in Smyrna I saw the same kind of earth, and brought some of it with me to England; it resembles musk in strength, but is more delicious in scent, and is not unlike the smell of a rose.

these compose the greater part of our household furniture. Houses so constructed and furnished require but little skill to erect them. Every man is a sufficient architect for the purpose. The whole neighborhood afford their unanimous assistance in building them, and in return receive and expect no other recompense than a feast.

As we live in a country where nature is prodigal of her favors, our wants are few and easily supplied; of course we have few manufactures. They consist for the most part of calicoes, earthen ware, ornaments, and instruments of war and husbandry. But these make no part of our commerce, the principal articles of which, as I have observed, are provisions. In such a state, money is of little use; however, we have some small pieces of coin, if I may call them such. They are made something like an anchor, but I do not remember either their value or denomination. We have also markets, at which I have been frequently with my mother. These are sometimes visited by stout mahogany-colored men from the south-west of us: we call them *Oye-Eboe,* which term signifies red men living at a distance. They generally bring us fire-arms, gunpowder, hats, beads, and dried fish. The last we esteemed a great rarity, as our waters were only brooks and springs. These articles they barter with us for odoriferous woods and earth, and our salt of wood ashes. They always carry slaves through our land; but the strictest account is exacted of their manner of procuring them before they are suffered to pass. Sometimes, indeed, we sold slaves to them, but they were only prisoners of war, or such among us as had been convicted of kidnapping, or adultery, and some other crimes, which we esteemed heinous. This practice of kidnapping induces me to think, that, notwithstanding all our strictness, their principal business among us was to trepan our people. I remember too, they carried great sacks along with them, which not long after, I had an opportunity of fatally seeing applied to that infamous purpose.

Our land is uncommonly rich and fruitful, and produces all kinds of vegetables in great abundance. We have plenty of Indian corn, and vast quantities of cotton and tobacco. Our pineapples grow without culture; they are about the size of the largest sugar-loaf, and finely flavored. We have also spices of different kinds, particularly pepper, and a variety of delicious fruits which I have never seen in Europe, together with gums of various kinds, and honey in abundance. All our industry is exerted to improve these blessings of nature. Agriculture is our chief employment; and everyone, even the children and women, are engaged in it. Thus we are all habituated to labor from our earliest years. Everyone contributes something to the common stock; and, as we are unacquainted with idleness, we have no beggars. The benefits of such a mode of living are obvious. The West India planters prefer the slaves of Benin or Eboe to those of any other part of Guinea, for their hardiness, intelligence, integrity, and zeal. Those benefits are felt by us in the general healthiness of the people, and in their vigor and activity; I might have added, too, in their comeliness. Deformity is indeed unknown amongst us, I mean that of shape. Numbers of the natives of Eboe now in London might be brought in support of this assertion: for, in regard to complexion, ideas of beauty are wholly relative. I remember while in Africa to have seen three Negro children who were tawny, and another quite white, who were universally regarded by myself, and the natives in general, as far as related to their complexions, as deformed. Our women, too, were, in my eye at least, uncommonly graceful, alert, and modest to a degree of bashfulness; nor do I remember to have heard of an instance of incontinence amongst them before marriage. They are also remarkably cheerful. Indeed, cheerfulness and affability are two of the leading characteristics of our nation.

Our tillage is exercised in a large plain or common, some hour's walk from our dwellings, and all the neighbors resort

1 An African village is invaded and men and women are captured for sale in the slave trade

thither in a body. They use no beasts of husbandry; and their only instruments are hoes, axes, shovels, and beaks, or pointed iron, to dig with. Sometimes we are visited by locusts, which come in large clouds, so as to darken the air, and destroy our harvest. This, however, happens rarely, but when it does, a famine is produced by it. I remember an instance or two wherein this happened. This common is often the theatre of war; and therefore when our people go out to till their land, they not only go in a body, but generally take their arms with them for fear of a surprise; and when they apprehend an invasion, they guard the avenues to their dwellings, by driving sticks into the ground, which are so sharp at one end as to pierce the foot, and are generally dipt in poison. From what I can recollect of these battles, they appear to have been irruptions of one little state or district on the other, to obtain prisoners or booty. Perhaps they were incited to this by those traders who brought the European goods I mentioned, amongst us. Such a mode of obtaining slaves in Africa is common; and I believe more are procured this way, and by kidnapping, than any other.* When a trader wants slaves, he applies to a chief for them, and tempts him with his wares. It is not extraordinary, if on this occasion he yields to the temptation with as little firmness, and accepts the price of his fellow creature's liberty with as little reluctance as the enlightened merchant. Accordingly he falls on his neighbors, and a desperate battle ensues. If he prevails and takes prisoners, he gratifies his avarice by selling them; but, if his party be vanquished, and he falls into the hands of the enemy, he is put to death; for, as he has been known to foment their quarrels, it is thought dangerous to let him survive, and no ransom can save him, though all other prisoners may be redeemed. We have fire-arms, bows and arrows, broad two-edged swords and javelins; we have shields also which cover a man from

* See Benezet's "Account of Africa," throughout.

head to foot. All are taught the use of these weapons; even our women are warriors, and march boldly out to fight along with the men. Our whole district is a kind of militia: on a certain signal given, such as the firing of a gun at night, they all rise in arms and rush upon their enemy. It is perhaps something remarkable, that when our people march to the field a red flag or banner is borne before them. I was once a witness to a battle in our common. We had been all at work in it one day as usual, when our people were suddenly attacked. I climbed a tree at some distance, from which I beheld the fight. There were many women as well as men on both sides; among others my mother was there, and armed with a broad sword. After fighting for a considerable time with great fury, and many had been killed, our people obtained the victory, and took their enemy's Chief a prisoner. He was carried off in great triumph, and, though he offered a large ransom for his life, he was put to death. A virgin of note among our enemies had been slain in the battle, and her arm was exposed in our marketplace, where our trophies were always exhibited. The spoils were divided according to the merit of the warriors. Those prisoners which were not sold or redeemed, we kept as slaves; but how different was their condition from that of the slaves in the West Indies! With us, they do no more work than other members of the community, even their master; their food, clothing, and lodging were nearly the same as theirs (except that they were not permitted to eat with those who were free-born); and there was scarce any other difference between them, than a superior degree of importance which the head of a family possesses in our state, and that authority which, as such, he exercises over every part of his household. Some of these slaves have even slaves under them as their own property, and for their own use.

As to religion, the natives believe that there is one Creator of all things, and that he lives in the sun. and is girted round with a belt; that he may never eat or drink, but, according to some, he smokes a pipe, which is our own favorite luxury. They believe he governs events, especially our deaths or captivity; but, as for the doctrine of eternity, I do not remember to have ever heard of it; some, however, believe in the transmigration of souls in a certain degree. Those spirits which were not transmigrated, such as their dear friends or relations, they believe always attend them, and guard them from the bad spirits or their foes. For this reason they always, before eating, as I have observed, put some small portion of the meat, and pour some of their drink, on the ground for them; and they often make oblations of the blood of beasts or fowls at their graves. I was very fond of my mother, and almost constantly with her. When she went to make these oblations at her mother's tomb, which was a kind of small solitary thatched house, I sometimes attended her. There she made her libations, and spent most of the night in cries and lamentations. I have been often extremely terrified on these occasions. The loneliness of the place, the darkness of the night, and the ceremony of libation, naturally awful and gloomy, were heightened by my mother's lamentations; and these concurring with the doleful cries of birds, by which these places were frequented, gave an inexpressible terror to the scene.

We compute the year, from the day on which the sun crosses the line, and on its setting that evening, there is a general shout throughout the land; at least, I can speak from my own knowledge, throughout our vicinity. The people at the same time make a great noise with rattles, not unlike the basket rattles used by children here, though much larger, and hold up their hands to heaven for a blessing. It is then the greatest offerings are made; and those children whom our wise men foretell will be fortunate are then presented to different people. I remember many used to come to see me, and I was carried about to others for that purpose. They have many offerings, particularly at full moons; generally two, at harvest, before the fruits are taken out of the ground; and when any young animals are killed, sometimes they offer up part of them as a sacrifice. These offerings, when made by one of the heads of a family, serve for the whole. I remember we often had them at my father's and my uncle's, and their families have been present. Some of our offerings are eaten with bitter herbs. We had a saying among us to anyone of a cross temper, "That if they were to be eaten, they should be eaten with bitter herbs."

We practised circumcision like the Jews, and made offerings and feasts on that occasion, in the same manner as they did. Like them also, our children were named from some event, some circumstance, or fancied foreboding, at the time of their birth. I was named *Olaudah,* which in our language signifies vicissitude, or fortunate; also, one favored, and having a loud voice and well spoken. I remember we never polluted the name of the object of our adoration; on the contrary, it was always mentioned with the greatest reverence; and we were totally unacquainted with swearing, and all those terms of abuse and reproach which find their way so readily and copiously into the language of more civilized people. The only expressions of that kind I remember were, "May you rot, or may you swell, or may a beast take you."

I have before remarked that the natives of this part of Africa are extremely cleanly. This necessary habit of decency was with us a part of religion, and therefore we had many purifications and washings; indeed almost as many, and used on the same occasions, if my recollection does not fail me, as the Jews. Those that touched the dead at any time were obliged to wash and purify themselves before they could enter a dwelling-house. Every woman, too, at certain times was forbidden to come into a dwelling-house, or touch any person, or anything we eat. I was so fond of my mother I could not keep from her, or avoid touching her at some of those periods, in consequence of which I was obliged to be kept out with her, in a little house made for that purpose, till offering was made, and then we were purified.

Though we had no places of public worship, we had priests and magicians, or wise men. I do not remember whether they had different offices, or whether they were united in the same persons, but they were held in great reverence by the people. They calculated our time, and foretold events, as their name imported, for we called them *Ah-affoe-way-cah,* which signifies calculators or yearly men, our year being called *Ah-affoe.* They wore their beards, and when they died, they were succeeded by their sons. Most of their implements and things of value were interred along with them. Pipes and tobacco were also put into the grave with the corpse, which was always perfumed and ornamented, and animals were offered in sacrifice to them. None accompanied their funerals, but those of the same profession or tribe. They buried them after sunset, and always returned from the grave by a different way from that which they went.

These magicians were also our doctors or physicians. They practised bleeding by cupping, and were very successful in healing wounds and expelling poisons. They had likewise some extraordinary method of discovering jealousy, theft, poisoning, the success of which, no doubt, they derived from the unbounded influence over the credulity and superstition of the people.

Chapter 2

My father, besides many slaves, had a numerous family, of which seven lived to grow up, including myself and sister, who was the only daughter. As I was the youngest of the sons, I became, of course, the greatest favorite with my mother, and was always with her; and she used to take particular pains to form my mind. I was trained up from my

earliest years in the art of war: my daily exercise was shooting and throwing javelins, and my mother adorned me with
emblems, after the manner of our greatest warriors. In this
way I grew up till I had turned the age of eleven, when an
end was put to my happiness in the following manner: Generally, when the grown people in the neighborhood were gone
far in the fields to labor, the children assembled together in
some of the neighboring premises to play; and commonly
some of us used to get up a tree to look out for any assailant,
or kidnapper, that might come upon us—for they sometimes
took those opportunities of our parents' absence, to attack
and carry off as many as they could seize. One day as I was
watching at the top of a tree in our yard, I saw one of those
people come into the yard of our next neighbor but one, to
kidnap, there being many stout young people in it. Immediately on this I gave the alarm of the rogue, and he was surrounded by the stoutest of them, who entangled him with
cords, so that he could not escape, till some of the grown
people came and secured him. But, alas! ere long it was my
fate to be thus attacked, and to be carried off, when none of
the grown people were nigh. One day, when all our people
were gone out to their works as usual, and only I and my
dear sister were left to mind the house, two men and a
woman got over our walls, and in a moment seized us both,
and, without giving us time to cry out, or make resistance,
they stopped our mouths, and ran off with us into the nearest
wood. Here they tied our hands, and continued to carry us as
far as they could, till night came on, when we reached a small
house, where the robbers halted for refreshment, and spent
the night. We were then unbound, but were unable to take
any food; and, being quite overpowered by fatigue and grief,
our only relief was some sleep, which allayed our misfortune
for a short time. The next morning we left the house, and continued travelling all the day. For a long time we had kept [to]
the woods, but at last we came into a road which I believed I

knew. I had now some hopes of being delivered; for we had advanced but a little way before I discovered some people at a distance, on which I began to cry out for their assistance; but my cries had no other effect than to make them tie me faster and stop my mouth, and then they put me into a large sack. They also stopped my sister's mouth, and tied her hands; and in this manner we proceeded till we were out of sight of these people. When we went to rest the following night, they offered us some victuals, but we refused it; and the only comfort we had was in being in one another's arms all that night, and bathing each other with our tears. But alas! we were soon deprived of even the small comfort of weeping together. The next day proved a day of greater sorrow than I had yet experienced; for my sister and I were then separated, while we lay clasped in each other's arms. It was in vain that we besought them not to part us; she was torn from me, and immediately carried away, while I was left in a state of distraction not to be described. I cried and grieved continually; and for several days did not eat anything but what they forced into my mouth. . . .

From the time I left my own nation, I always found somebody that understood me till I came to the sea coast. The languages of different nations did not totally differ, nor were they so copious as those of the Europeans, particularly the English. They were therefore, easily learned; and, while I was journeying thus through Africa, I acquired two or three different tongues. In this manner I had been travelling for a considerable time, when, one evening, to my great surprise, whom should I see brought to the house where I was but my dear sister! As soon as she saw me, she gave a loud shriek, and ran into my arms—I was quite overpowered; neither of us could speak, but, for a considerable time, clung to each other in mutual embraces, unable to do anything but weep. Our meeting affected all who saw us; and, indeed, I must acknowledge, in honor of those sable destroyers of human rights, that I never met with any ill treatment, or saw any offered to their slaves, except tying them, when necessary, to keep them from running away. When these people knew we were brother and sister, they indulged us to be together; and the man, to whom I supposed we belonged, lay with us, he in the middle, while she and I held one another by the hands across his breast all night; and thus for a while we forgot our misfortunes, in the joy of being together; but even this small comfort was soon to have an end; for scarcely had the fatal morning appeared when she was again torn from me forever! I was now more miserable, if possible, than before. The small relief which her presence gave me from pain, was gone, and the wretchedness of my situation was redoubled by my anxiety after her fate, and my apprehensions lest her sufferings should be greater than mine, when I could not be with her to alleviate them. . . .

I did not long remain after my sister. I was again sold, and carried through a number of places, till after travelling a considerable time, I came to a town called Tinmah, in the most beautiful country I had yet seen in Africa. It was extremely rich, and there were many rivulets which flowed through it, and supplied a large pond in the centre of the town, where the people washed. Here I first saw and tasted cocoanuts, which I thought superior to any nuts I had ever tasted before; and the trees, which were loaded, were also interspersed among the houses, which had commodious shades adjoining, and were in the same manner as ours, the insides being neatly plastered and whitewashed. Here I also saw and tasted for the first time, sugar cane. Their money consisted of little white shells, the size of the finger nail. I was sold here for one hundred and seventy-two of them, by a merchant who lived and brought me there. I had been about two or three days at his house, when a wealthy widow, a neighbor of his, came there one evening, and brought with her an only son, a young gentleman about my own age and size. Here

they saw me; and, having taken a fancy to me, I was bought
of the merchant, and went home with them. Her house and
premises were situated close to one of those rivulets I have
mentioned, and were the finest I ever saw in Africa: they
were very extensive, and she had a number of slaves to
attend her. The next day I was washed and perfumed, and
when meal time came, I was led into the presence of my
mistress, and ate and drank before her with her son. This
filled me with astonishment; and I could scarce help expressing my surprise that the young gentleman should suffer me,
who was bound, to eat with him who was free; and not only
so, but that he would not at any time either eat or drink till
I had taken first, because I was the eldest, which was agreeable to our custom. Indeed, every thing here, and all their
treatment of me, made me forget that I was a slave. The
language of these people resembled ours so nearly, that we
understood each other perfectly. They had also the very same
customs as we. There were likewise slaves daily to attend us,
while my young master and I, with other boys, sported with
our darts and bows and arrows, as I had been used to do at
home. In this resemblance to my former happy state, I passed
about two months; and I now began to think I was to be
adopted into the family, and was beginning to be reconciled
to my situation, and to forget by degrees my misfortunes,
when all at once the delusion vanished; for, without the least
previous knowledge, one morning early, while my dear master
and companion was still asleep, I was awakened out of my
reverie to fresh sorrow, and hurried away even amongst the
uncircumcised. . . .

Thus I continued to travel, sometimes by land, sometimes
by water, through different countries and various nations, till,
at the end of six or seven months after I had been kidnapped,
I arrived at the sea coast. . . .

The first object which saluted my eyes when I arrived on
the coast, was the sea, and a slave ship, which was then riding

at anchor, and waiting for its cargo. These filled me with astonishment, which was soon converted into terror, when I was carried on board. I was immediately handled, and tossed up to see if I were sound, by some of the crew; and I was now persuaded that I had gotten into a world of bad spirits, and that they were going to kill me. Their complexions, too, differing so much from ours, their long hair, and the language they spoke (which was very different from any I had ever heard), united to confirm me in this belief. Indeed, such were the horrors of my views and fears at the moment, that, if ten thousand worlds had been my own, I would have freely parted with them all to have exchanged my condition with that of the meanest slave in my own country. When I looked round the ship too, and saw a large furnace of copper boiling, and a multitude of black people of every description chained together, every one of their countenances expressing dejection and sorrow, I no longer doubted of my fate; and, quite overpowered with horror and anguish, I fell motionless on the deck and fainted. When I recovered a little, I found some black people about me, who I believed were some of those who had brought me on board, and had been receiving their pay; they talked to me in order to cheer me, but in vain. I asked them if we were not to be eaten by those white men with horrible looks, red faces, and long hair. They told me I was not, and one of the crew brought me a small portion of spirituous liquor in a wine glass; but, being afraid of him, I would not take it out of his hand. One of the blacks, therefore, took it from him and gave it to me, and I took a little down my palate, which, instead of reviving me, as they thought it would, threw me into the greatest consternation at the strange feeling it produced, having never tasted any such liquor before. Soon after this, the blacks who brought me on board went off, and left me abandoned to despair.

I now saw myself deprived of all chance of returning to my native country, or even the least glimpse of hope of gaining the shore, which I now considered as friendly; and I even wished for my former slavery in preference to my present situation, which was filled with horrors of every kind, still heightened by my ignorance of what I was to undergo. I was not long suffered to indulge my grief; I was soon put down under the decks, and there I received such a salutation in my nostrils as I had never experienced in my life: so that, with the loathsomeness of the stench, and crying together, I became so sick and low that I was not able to eat, nor had I the least desire to taste anything. I now wished for the last friend, death, to relieve me; but soon, to my grief, two of the white men offered me eatables; and, on my refusing to eat, one of them held me fast by the hands, and laid me across, I think, the windlass, and tied my feet, while the other flogged me severely. I had never experienced anything of this kind before, and, although not being used to the water, I naturally feared that element the first time I saw it, yet, nevertheless, could I have got over the nettings, I would have jumped over the side, but I could not; and besides, the crew used to watch us very closely who were not chained down to the decks, lest we should leap into the water; and I have seen some of these poor African prisoners most severely cut, for attempting to do so, and hourly whipped for not eating. This indeed was often the case with myself. In a little time after, amongst the poor chained men, I found some of my own nation, which in a small degree gave ease to my mind. I inquired of these what was to be done with us? They gave me to understand, we were to be carried to these white people's country to work for them. I then was a little revived, and thought, if it were no worse than working, my situation was not so desperate; but still I feared I should be put to death, the white people looked and acted, as I thought, in so savage a manner; for I had never seen among any people such instances of brutal cruelty; and this not only shown towards us blacks, but also to some of the whites themselves. One white man in particu-

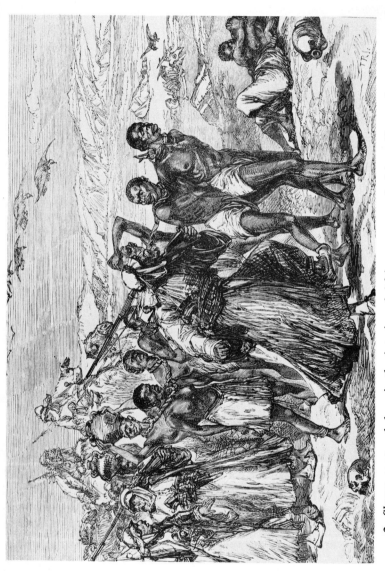

2 Slaves captured deep in the interior of Africa were marched in coffles to the port cities, and bought and sold by the European companies conducting the commerce in slaves

lar I saw, when we were permitted to be on deck, flogged so unmercifully with a large rope near the foremast, that he died in consequence of it; and they tossed him over the side as they would have done a brute. This made me fear these people the more; and I expected nothing less than to be treated in the same manner. I could not help expressing my fears and apprehensions to some of my countrymen; I asked them if these people had no country, but lived in this hollow place (the ship)? They told me they did not, but came from a distant one. "Then," said I, "how comes it in all our country we never heard of them?" They told me because they lived so very far off. I then asked where were their women? Had they any like themselves? I was told they had. "And why," said I "do we not see them?" They answered, because they were left behind. I asked how the vessel could go? They told me they could not tell; but that there was cloth put upon the masts by the help of the ropes I saw, and then the vessel went on; and the white men had some spell or magic they put in the water when they liked, in order to stop the vessel. I was exceedingly amazed at this account, and really thought they were spirits. I therefore wished much to be from amongst them, for I expected they would sacrifice me; but my wishes were vain—for we were so quartered that it was impossible for any of us to make our escape.

While we stayed on the coast I was mostly on deck; and one day, to my great astonishment, I saw one of these vessels coming in with the sails up. As soon as the whites saw it, they gave a great shout, at which we were amazed; and the more so, as the vessel appeared larger by approaching nearer. At last, she came to an anchor in my sight, and when the anchor was let go, I and my countrymen who saw it, were lost in astonishment to observe the vessel stop—and were now convinced it was done by magic. Soon after this the other ship got her boats out, and they came on board of us, and the people of both ships seemed very glad to see each other. Several of the strangers also shook hands with us black people, and made motions with their hands, signifying I suppose, we were to go to their country, but we did not understand them.

At last, when the ship we were in, had got in all her cargo, they made ready with many fearful noises, and we were all put under deck, so that we could not see how they managed the vessel. But this disappointment was the least of my sorrow. The stench of the hold while we were on the coast was so intolerably loathsome, that it was dangerous to remain there for any time, and some of us had been permitted to stay on the deck for the fresh air; but now that the whole ship's cargo were confined together, it became absolutely pestilential. The closeness of the place, and the heat of the climate, added to the number in the ship, which was so crowded that each had scarcely room to turn himself, almost suffocated us. This produced copious perspirations, so that the air soon became unfit for respiration, from a variety of loathsome smells, and brought on a sickness among the slaves, of which many died—thus falling victims to the improvident avarice, as I may call it, of their purchasers. This wretched situation was again aggravated by the galling of the chains, now became insupportable, and the filth of the necessary tubs, into which the children often fell, and were almost suffocated. The shrieks of the women, and the groans of the dying, rendered the whole a scene of horror almost inconceivable. Happily perhaps, for myself, I was soon reduced so low here that it was thought necessary to keep me almost always on deck; and for my extreme youth I was not put in fetters. In this situation I expected every hour to share the fate of my companions, some of whom were almost daily brought upon deck at the point of death, which I began to hope would soon put an end to my miseries. Often did I think many of the inhabitants of the deep much more happy than myself. I envied them the freedom they enjoyed, and as often wished I could change my condition for theirs. Every circumstance I met with, served only to render my state more painful, and heightened my apprehensions, and my opinion of the cruelty of the whites.

One day they had taken a number of fishes; and when they had killed and satisfied themselves with as many as they thought fit, to our astonishment who were on deck, rather than give any of them to us to eat, as we expected, they tossed the remaining fish into the sea again, although we begged and prayed for some as well as we could, but in vain; and some of my countrymen, being pressed by hunger, took an opportunity, when they thought no one saw them of trying to get a little privately; but they were discovered, and the attempt procured them some very severe floggings. One day, when we had a smooth sea and moderate wind, two of my wearied countrymen who were chained together (I was near them at the time), preferring death to such a life of misery, somehow made through the nettings and jumped into the sea; immediately, another quite dejected fellow, who, on account of his illness, was suffered to be out of irons; also followed their example; and I believe many more would very soon have done the same, if they had not been prevented by the ship's crew, who were instantly alarmed. Those of us that were the most active, were in a moment put down under the deck; and there was such a noise and confusion amongst the people of the ship as I never heard before, to stop her, and get the boat out to go after the slaves. However, two of the wretches were drowned, but they got the other, and afterwards flogged him unmercifully, for thus attempting to prefer death to slavery. In this manner we continued to undergo more hardships than I can now relate, hardships which are inseparable from this accursed trade. Many a time we were near suffocation from the want of fresh air, which we were often without for whole days together. This, and the stench of the necessary tubs, carried off many.

During our passage, I first saw flying fishes, which sur-prised me very much; they used frequently to fly across the ship, and many of them fell on the deck. I also now first saw the use of the quadrant; I had often with astonishment seen the mariners make observations with it, and I could not think what it meant. They at last took notice of my surprise; and one of them, willing to increase it, as well as to gratify my curiosity, made me one day look through it. The clouds appeared to me to be land, which disappeared as they passed along. This heightened my wonder; and I was now more persuaded than ever, that I was in another world, and that every thing about me was magic. At last, we came in sight of the island of Barbadoes, at which the whites on board gave a great shout, and made many signs of joy to us. We did not know what to think of this; but as the vessel drew nearer, we plainly saw the harbor, and other ships of different kinds and sizes, and we soon anchored amongst them, off Bridgetown. Many merchants and planters now came aboard, though it was in the evening. They put us in separate parcels, and examined us attentively. They also made us jump, and pointed to the land, signifying we were to go there. We thought by this, we should be eaten by these ugly men, as they appeared to us; and, when soon after we were all put down under the deck again, there was much dread and trembling among us, and nothing but bitter cries to be heard all the night from these apprehensions, insomuch, that at last the white people got some old slaves from the land to pacify us. They told us we were not to be eaten, but to work, and were soon to go on land, where we should see many of our country people. This report eased us much. And sure enough, soon after we were landed, there came to us Africans of all languages.

We were conducted immediately to the merchant's yard, where we were all pent up together, like so many sheep in a fold, without regard to sex or age. As every object was new to me, everything I saw filled me with surprise. What struck me first, was, that the houses were built with bricks and stories, and in every other respect different from those I had seen in Africa; but I was still more astonished on seeing people on horseback. I did not know what this could mean; and indeed, I thought these people were full of nothing but magical arts. While I was in this astonishment, one of my fellow prisoners spoke to a countryman of his, about the horses, who said they were the same kind they had in their country. I understood them, though they were from a distant part of Africa; and I thought it odd I had not seen any horses there; but afterwards, when I came to converse with different Africans, I found they had many horses amongst them, and much larger than those I then saw.

We were not many days in the merchant's custody, before we were sold after their usual manner, which is this: On a signal given (as the beat of a drum), the buyers rush at once into the yard where the slaves are confined, and make choice of that parcel they liked best. The noise and clamor with which this is attended, and the eagerness visible in the countenances of the buyers, serve not a little to increase the apprehension of terrified Africans, who may well be supposed to consider them as the ministers of that destruction to which they think themselves devoted. In this manner, without scruple, are relations and friends separated, most of them never to see each other again. I remember, in the vessel in which I was brought over, in the men's apartment, there were several brothers, who, in the sale, were sold in different lots; and it was very moving on this occasion, to see and hear their cries at parting. O, ye nominal Christians! might not an African ask you—Learned you this from your God, who says unto you, Do unto all men as you would men should do unto you? Is it not enough that we are torn from our country and friends, to toil for your luxury and lust of gain? Must every tender feeling be likewise sacrificed to your avarice? Are the dearest friends and relations, now rendered more dear by their separation from their kindred, still to be parted from each other, and thus prevented from cheering the gloom of slavery, with the small comfort of being together, and mingling their sufferings and sorrows? Why are parents to lose their children, brothers their sisters, or husbands their wives? Surely, this is a new refinement in cruelty, which, while it has no advantage to atone for it, thus aggravates distress, and adds fresh horrors even to the wretchedness of slavery.

OTTOBAH CUGOANO

At an early age Ottobah Cugoano was stolen away from Africa and sold into slavery in the West Indies. Most of the slaves brought to the West Indies were sold to the plantations in the Caribbean Islands and in the United States. Some were bought to be used as servants in England. Cugoano was liberated from slavery in Granada and taken to England by Lord Hoth where he was placed as a servant. He later entered the service of Richard Cosway, artist of the Royal Academy, and first painter of the Prince of Wales. In England he acquired the opportunities for self-education. In 1787, he published a little book in London entitled *Thoughts and Sentiments on the Evil and Wicked Traffic of the Slavery and Commerce of the Human Species, Humbly Submitted to the Inhabitants of Great-Britain*. It was primarily an impassioned argument against slavery, but it included a brief narrative of his life. His reference in his story to a factory should not occasion any surprise. Not all slaves worked on plantations. Quite a few labored in early manufacturing and industrial establishments, sometimes hired out by their owners to manufacturers and craftsmen and sometimes owned by manufacturers in the cities.

"I Was Early Snatched Away from My Native Country"

I was early snatched away from my native country, with about eighteen or twenty more boys and girls, as we were playing in a field. We lived but a few days' journey from the coast where we were kidnapped, and as we were decoyed

29

3 The road to the slave ships was a death road for many Africans
who never lived to suffer the transatlantic crossing

and drove along, we were soon conducted to a factory, and from thence, in the fashionable way of traffic, consigned to Grenada. Perhaps it may not be amiss to give a few remarks, as some account of myself, in this transposition of captivity.

I was born in the city of Agimaque, on the coast of Fantyn; my father was a companion to the chief in that part of the country of Fantee, and when the old king died I was left in his house with his family; soon after I was sent for by his nephew, Ambro Accasa, who succeeded the old king in the chiefdom of that part of Fantee, known by the name of Agimaque and Assince. I lived with his children, enjoying peace and tranquility, about twenty moons, which, according to their way of reckoning time, is two years. I was sent for to visit an uncle, who lived at a considerable distance from Agimaque. The first day after we set out we arrived at Assince, and the third day at my uncle's habitation, where I lived about three months, and was then thinking of returning to my father and young companion at Agimaque; but by this time I had got well acquainted with some of the children of my uncle's hundreds of relations, and we were some days too venturesome in going into the woods to gather fruit and catch birds, and such amusements as pleased us. One day I refused to go with the rest, being rather apprehensive that something might happen to us, till one of my playfellows said to me, "Because you belong to the great men, you are afraid to venture your carcase, or else of the *bounsam*," which is the devil. This enraged me so much, that I set a resolution to join the rest, and we went into the woods, as usual; but we had not been above two hours, before our troubles began, when several great ruffians came upon us suddenly, and said we had committed a fault against their lord, and we must go and answer for it ourselves before him.

Some of us attempted, in vain, to run away, but pistols and cutlasses were soon introduced, threatening, that if we offered to stir, we should all lie dead on the spot. One of them pretended to be more friendly than the rest, and said that he would speak to their lord to get us clear, and desired that we should follow him; we were then immediately divided into different parties, and drove after him. We were soon led out of the way which we knew, and towards evening, as we came in sight of a town, they told us that this great man of theirs lived there, but pretended it was too late to go and see him that night. Next morning there came three other men, whose language differed from ours, and spoke to some of those who watched us all the night; but he that pretended to be our friend with the great man, and some others, were gone away. We asked our keeper what these men had been saying to them, and they answered, that they had been asking them and us together to go and feast with them that day, and that we must put off seeing the great man till after, little thinking that our doom was so nigh, or that these villains meant to feast on us as their prey. We went with them again about half a day's journey, and came to a great multitude of people, having different music playing; and all the day after we got there, we were very merry with the music, dancing, and singing. Towards the evening, we were again persuaded that we could not get back to where the great man lived till next day, and when bed-time came, we were separated into different houses with different people. When the next morning came, I asked for the men that brought me there, and for the rest of my companions; and I was told that they were gone to the sea-side, to bring home some rum, guns, and powder; and that some of my companions were gone with them, and that some were gone to the fields to do something or other. This gave me strong suspicion that there was some treachery in the case, and I began to think that my hopes of returning home again were all over. I soon became very uneasy, not knowing what to do, and refused to eat or drink, for whole days together, till the man of the house told me that he would do all in his power to get me back to my uncle; then I eat a little fruit with him, and had some thoughts that I should be sought after, as I would be then missing at home about five or six days. I inquired every day if the men had come back, and for the rest of my companions, but could get no answer of any satisfaction. I was kept about six days at this man's house, and in the evening there was another man came, and talked with him a good while, and I heard the one say to the other he must go, and the other said, the sooner the better; that man came out and told me that he knew my relations at Agimaque, and that we must set out to-morrow morning, and he would convey me there. Accordingly we set out next day, and travelled till dark, when we came to a place where we had some supper and slept. He carried a large bag, with some gold dust, which he said he had to buy some goods at the sea-side to take with him to Agimaque. Next day we travelled on, and in the evening came to a town, where I saw several white people, which made me afraid that they would eat me, according to our notion, as children, in the inland parts of the country. This made me rest very uneasy all the night, and next morning I had some victuals brought, desiring me to eat and make haste, as my guide and kidnapper told me that he had to go to the castle with some company that were going there, as he had told me before, to get some goods. After I was ordered out, the horrors I soon saw and felt, cannot be well described; I saw many of my miserable countrymen chained two and two, some handcuffed, and some with their hands tied behind. We were conducted along by a guard, and when we arrived at the castle, I asked my guide what I was brought there for, he told me to learn the ways of the *browfow*, that is, the white-faced people. I saw him take a gun, a piece of cloth, and some lead for me, and then he told me that he must now leave me there, and went off. This made me cry bitterly, but I was soon conducted to a prison, for three days, where I heard the groans and cries of many, and saw some of my fellow-captives. But when a vessel arrived to conduct us away

4 The sketch, by a British lieutenant, depicts the slave market in Zanzibar, one of the many stations of the slave trade which was a key factor in the commercial expansion of Europe and the colonization of the New World

to the ship, it was a most horrible scene; there was nothing to be heard but the rattling of chains, smacking of whips, and the groans and cries of our fellow-men. Some would not stir from the ground, when they were lashed and beat in the most horrible manner. I have forgot the name of this infernal fort; but we were taken in the ship that came for us, to another that was ready to sail from Cape Coast. When we were put into the ship, we saw several black merchants coming on board, but we were all drove into our holes, and not suffered to speak to any of them. In this situation we continued several days in sight of our native-land; but I could find no good person to give any information of my situation to Accasa at Agimaque. And when we found ourselves at last taken away, death was more preferable than life; and a plan was concerted amongst us, that we might burn and blow up the ship, and to perish all together in the flames: but we were betrayed by one of our own countrywomen, who slept with some of the headmen of the ship, for it was common for the dirty filthy sailors to take the African women and lie upon their bodies; but the men were chained and pent up in holes. It was the women and boys which were to burn the ship, with the approbation and groans of the rest; though that was prevented, the discovery was likewise a cruel bloody scene.

But it would be needless to give a description of all the horrible scenes which we saw, and the base treatment which we met with in this dreadful captive situation, as the similar cases of thousands, which suffer by this infernal traffic, are well known. Let it suffice to say that I was thus lost to my dear indulgent parents and relations, and they to me. All my help was cries and tears, and these could not avail, nor suffered long, till one succeeding woe and dread swelled up another. Brought from a state of innocence and freedom, and, in a barbarous and cruel manner, conveyed to a state of horror and slavery, this abandoned situation may be easier conceived than described. From the time that I was kidnapped, and conducted to a factory, and from thence in the brutish, base, but fashionable way of traffic, consigned to Grenada, the grievous thoughts which I then felt, still pant in my heart; though my fears and tears have long since subsided. And yet it is still grievous to think that thousands more have suffered in similar and greater distress, under the hands of barbarous robbers, and merciless task-masters; and that many, even now, are suffering in all the extreme bitterness of grief and woe, that no language can describe. The cries of some, and the sight of their misery, may be seen and heard afar; but the deep-sounding groans of thousands, and the great sadness of their misery and woe, under the heavy load of oppressions and calamities inflicted upon them, are such as can only be distinctly known to the ears of Jehovah Sabaoth.

This Lord of Hosts, in his great providence, and in great mercy to me, made a way for my deliverance from Grenada. Being in this dreadful captivity and horrible slavery, without any hope of deliverance, for about eight or nine months, beholding the most dreadful scenes of misery and cruelty, and seeing my miserable companions often cruelly lashed, and, as it were, cut to pieces, for the most trifling faults; this made me often tremble and weep, but I escaped better than many of them. For eating a piece of sugar-cane, some were cruelly lashed, or struck over the face, to knock their teeth out. Some of the stouter ones, I suppose, often reproved, and grown hardened and stupid with many cruel beatings and lashings, or perhaps faint and pressed with hunger and hard labor, were often committing trespasses of this kind, and when detected, they met with exemplary punishment. Some told me they had their teeth pulled out, to deter others, and to prevent them from eating any cane in future. Thus seeing my miserable companions and countrymen in this pitiful, distressed, and horrible situation, with all the brutish baseness and barbarity attending it, could not but fill my little mind with horror and indignation. But I must own, to the shame of my own countrymen, that I was first kidnapped and betrayed by some of my own complexion, who were the first cause of my exile and slavery; but if there were no buyers there would be no sellers. So far as I can remember, some of the Africans in my country keep slaves, which they take in war, or for debt; but those which they keep are well fed, and good care taken of them, and treated well; and as to their clothing, they differ according to the custom of the country. But I may safely say, that all the poverty and misery that any of the inhabitants of Africa meet with among themselves, is far inferior to those inhospitable regions of misery which they meet with in the West-Indies, where their hard-hearted overseers have neither regard to the laws of God, nor the life of their fellow-men.

Thanks be to God, I was delivered from Grenada, and that horrid brutal slavery. A gentleman coming to England took me for his servant, and brought me away, where I soon found my situation become more agreeable. After coming to England, and seeing others write and read, I had a strong desire to learn, and getting what assistance I could, I applied myself to learn reading and writing, which soon became my recreation, pleasure, and delight; and when my master perceived that I could write some, he sent me to a proper school for that purpose to learn. Since, I have endeavoured to improve my mind in reading, and have sought to get all the intelligence I could, in my situation of life, towards the state of my brethren and countrymen in complexion, and of the miserable situation of those who are barbarously sold into captivity, and unlawfully held in slavery.

BELINDA

Belinda is the only name we have for the African woman who addressed the following petition to the Legislature of the State of Massachusetts in 1782, shortly after the American War of Independence. She was captured in Africa as a child and was sold into slavery in the British colonies in North America. Shortly after the War of Independence, Belinda submitted a petition to the government of Massachusetts claiming her rights, in her older age, to some of the fruit of her years of toil and servitude. It is not a slave narrative, strictly speaking, but all that we know of the story of her life is embodied in this petition. It is reproduced exactly as it was published in the famous eighteenth-century Philadelphia publication *The American Museum or Repository of Ancient and Modern Fugitive Pieces, &c. Prose and Poetical*, Vol. I, Number VI, June, 1787. The style and language show signs of literary editing, but the point of view clearly reflects the atitudes of an African woman forced into slavery in exile. Her memories of Africa are particularly striking.

"The Cruelty of Men, Whose Faces Were Like the Moon"

PETITION OF AN AFRICAN SLAVE, TO THE LEGISLATURE OF MASSACHUSETTS

To the honourable the Senate and house of representatives, in general court assembled:

THE PETITION OF BELINDA, AN AFRICAN,
HUMBLY SHEWS,

That seventy years have rolled away, since she, on the banks
of the Rio de Valta, received her existence. The mountains,
covered with spicy forests—valleys, loaded with the richest
fruits spontaneously produced—joined to that happy tempera-
ture of air, which excludes excess, would have yielded her
the soft complete felicity, had not her mind received early
impressions of the cruelty of men, whose faces were like the
moon, and whose bows and arrows were like the thunder and
the lightning of the clouds. The idea of these, the most dreadful of all enemies, filled her infant slumbers with horror, and
her noon-tide moments with cruel apprehensions! But her
affrighted imagination, in its most alarming extension, never
represented distresses equal to what she has since really
experienced: for before she had twelve years enjoyed the
fragrance of her native groves, and ere she had realized that
Europeans placed their happiness in yellow dust, which she
carelessly marked with her infant footsteps—even when she,
in a sacred grove, with each hand in that of a tender parent,
was paying her devotion to the great Orisa, who made all
things, an armed band of white men, driving many of her
countrymen in chains, rushed into the hallowed shades!
Could the tears, the sighs, the supplications, bursting from
the tortured parental affection, have blunted the keen edge
of avarice, she might have been rescued from agony, which
many of her country's children have felt, but which none
have ever described. In vain she lifted her supplicating voice
to an insulted father, and her guiltless hands to a dishonoured
deity! She was ravished from the bosom of her country, from
the arms of her friends, while the advanced age of her parents rendering them unfit for servitude, cruelly separated her
from them for ever.

Scenes which her imagination had never conceived of, a
floating world, the sporting monsters of the deep, and the

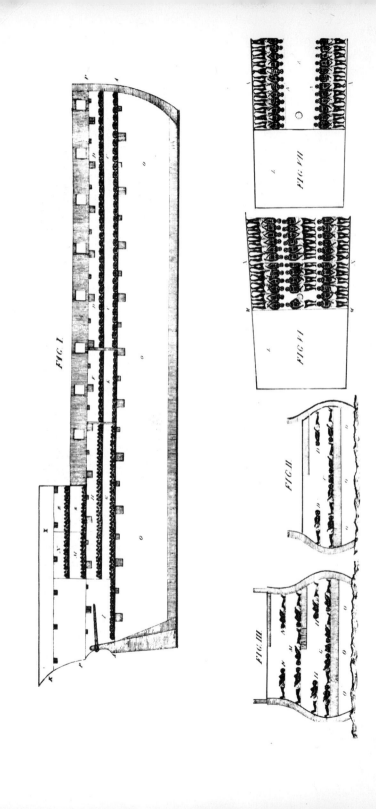

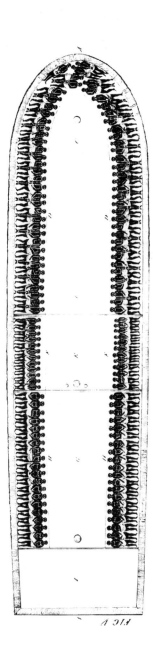

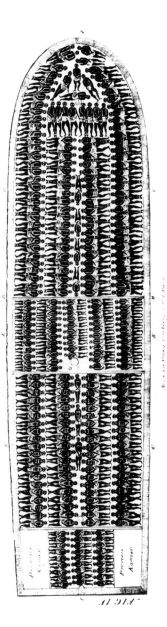

5 In the slave ships, slaves were crowded together with barely room for standing, lying down, or sitting, and many never survived the Atlantic journey. This is the loading plan of the *Brookes* (1839)

familiar meetings of billows and clouds, strove, but in vain, to divert her attention from three hundred Africans in chains, suffering the most excruciating torment; and some of them rejoicing that the pangs of death came like a balm to their wounds.

Once more her eyes were blest with a continent: but alas! how unlike the land where she received her being! Here all things appeared unpropitious. She learned to catch the ideas, marked by the sounds of language, only to know that her doom was slavery, from which death alone was to emancipate. What did it avail her, that the walls of her lord were hung with splendor, and that the dust trodden under foot in her native country, crowded his gates with sordid worshippers! The laws rendered her incapable of receiving property: and though she was a free moral agent, accountable for her own actions, yet never she had a moment at her own disposal! Fifty years her faithful hands have been compelled to ignoble servitude for the benefit of an Isaac Royall, until, as if nations must be agitated, and the world convulsed, for the preservation of that freedom, which the Almighty Father intended for all the human race, the present war commenced. The terrors of men, armed in the cause of freedom, compelled her master to fly, and to breathe away his life in a land, where lawless dominion sits enthroned, pouring blood and vengeance on all who dare to be free.

The face of your petitioner is now marked with the furrows of time, and her frame feebly bending under the oppression of years, while she, by the laws of the land, is denied the enjoyment of one morsel of that immense wealth, a part whereof hath been accumulated by her own industry, and the whole augmented by her servitude.

Wherefore, casting herself at the feet of your honours, as to a body of men, formed for the extirpation of vassalage, for the reward of virtue, and the just returns of honest industry— she prays that such allowance may be made her, out of the estate of colonel Royall, as will prevent her, and her more infirm daughter, from misery in the greatest extreme, and scatter comfort over the short and downward path of their lives: and she will ever pray.

BELINDA.

Boston, February, 1782.

IGNATIUS SANCHO

Ignatius Sancho was the first African born in slavery to acquire recognition as a man of letters in eighteenth-century England. His father and mother were captured in Africa and he was born aboard a slave ship, in 1729, during the transatlantic passage. When the ship arrived at Carthagena, in South America, he was baptized Ignatius. His mother died shortly afterward and his father killed himself rather than serve as a slave. The infant was bought by a man who took him to England and gave him as a gift to three unmarried sisters who lived at Greenwich. The Duke of Montagu lived in the neighbourhood and became acquainted with the young African. The Duke was impressed by his intelligence and wit, introduced him to the Duchess, and they encouraged him to learn to read and write and lent him books. He entered service as a butler in the home of the Montagu family and worked for them for more than twenty years. When he was in his forties he finally set up a small shop for groceries. He was an avid reader, conversationalist, and letter-writer, and in 1782, two years after his death, a two-volume book entitled *Letters of Ignatius Sancho,* edited by Joseph Jekyll, was published in London. The book aroused considerable interest and was subsequently republished in a number of editions. Sancho had never intended these letters for publication and did not keep copies of them. The book was edited and produced from original copies of the letters in the possession of their recipients. One of the letters was addressed to Reverend Laurence Sterne, the author of *Tristram Shandy.* In the book this letter was dated July, 1776, but this is an error because Sterne died in 1768, and wrote an answer to Ignatius Sancho, dated July 27, 1766, which was the actual year of Sancho's letter to him. In his reply to Ignatius Sancho, Laurence Sterne wrote:

There is a strange coincidence, Sancho, in the little events of this world, as well as the great ones. I had been writing a tender tale of the sorrows of a poor, friendless negro girl, and my eyes had scarce done smarting with it, when your letter, in behalf of so many of her brethren and sisters, came to me. But why *her* brethren or *your* brethren, Sancho, any more than *mine*? It is by the finest tints, and the most insensible gradations, that nature descends from the fairest face to the sootiest complexion. At which of these tints are the ties of blood to cease? And how many shades lower in the scale must we descend ere mercy is to vanish with them?

It is no uncommon thing, my good Sancho, for one half of the world to *use* the other half like brutes, and then endeavor to *make* them so. For my part, I never look Westward, when I am in a pensive mood, without thinking of the burdens our brothers and sisters are there carrying. If I could ease their shoulders from one ounce of them, I declare I would this hour set out upon a pilgrimage to Mecca for their sakes. It casts a sad shade upon the world that so great a part of it are, and have so long been, bound in chains of darkness and chains of misery.

"A Tear in Favour of My Miserable Black Brethren"

TO MR. STERNE.

July, 1776.

REVEREND SIR,

It would be an insult on your humanity (or perhaps look like it) to apologize for the liberty I am taking.—I am one of those people whom the vulgar and illiberal call *"Negurs."*—The first part of my life was rather unlucky, as I was placed in a family

6 This engraving, attributed to William Blake, depicts a group of
slaves imported to be sold in the British West Indies. The slave trade
lasted for more than three centuries, and about 20 million Africans
were forcibly transported across the Atlantic

who judged ignorance the best and only security for obedience.—A little reading and writing I got by unwearied application.—The latter part of my life has been—thro' God's blessing, truly fortunate, having spent it in the service of one of the best families in the kingdom.—My chief pleasure has been books.— Philanthropy I adore.—How very much, good Sir, am I (amongst millions) indebted to you for the character of your amiable uncle Toby!—I declare, I would walk ten miles in the dog-days, to shake hands with the honest corporal.—Your Sermons have touch'd me to the heart, and I hope have amended it, which brings me to the point.—In your tenth discourse, page seventy-eight, in the second volume—is this very affecting passage—"Consider how great a part of our species—in all ages down to this—have been trod under the feet of cruel and capricious tyrants, who would neither hear their cries, nor pity their distresses.—Consider slavery—what it is—how bitter a draught—and how many millions are made to drink it!"—Of all my favourite authors, not one has drawn a tear in favour of my miserable black brethren—excepting yourself, and the humane author of Sir George Ellison.—I think you will forgive me;—I am sure you will applaud me for beseeching you to give one half hour's attention to slavery, as it is at this day practised in our West Indies.—That subject, handled in your striking manner, would ease the yoke (perhaps) of many—but if only of one—Gracious God!—what a feast to a benevolent heart!— and, sure I am, you are an epicurean in acts of charity.—You, who are universally read, and as universally admired—you could not fail—Dear Sir, think in me you behold the uplifted hands of thousands of my brother Moors.—Grief (you pathetically observe) is eloquent;—figure to yourself their attitudes;—hear their supplicating addresses!—alas!—you cannot refuse.—Humanity must comply—in which hope I beg permission to subscribe myself,

Reverend, Sir, &c.

I. SANCHO.

AUSTIN STEWARD

Twenty-two Years a Slave, and Forty Years a Freeman was the title of the autobiographical narrative by Austin Steward, first published in Rochester, New York, in 1857. Its author was born a slave on a plantation in Virginia in the early 1790s. Most slaves did not know their exact dates of birth. The owner later migrated to western New York State and brought all of his slaves along with him. The former plantation-owner became a businessman in the North and he hired out his slaves for wages that were paid to the owner. Austin Steward was hired out in this fashion, but after some time he became familiar with the manumission laws and court rulings that preceded the final legal abolition of slavery in New York State and secured his freedom by his own efforts. In 1815, Steward refused to let himself be hired out for wages to be paid to his so-called owner on the grounds that it was a violation of the judicial interpretation that this practice was an evasion of an earlier manumission law. He acquired the status of a free Negro and began to hire his services out independently. In his narrative he depicted his early life as a slave as well as his life as a free Negro in the North. Steward's book was thus not only a slave narrative but also a portrayal of the conditions of life of free Negroes in the North. In the concluding chapter of his narrative he wrote:

> For many years past, I have been a close and interested observer of my race, both free and enslaved. I have observed with great pleasure, the gradual improvement in intelligence and condition of the free colored people of the North. In proportion as prejudice has diminished, they have gradually advanced . . . That prejudice against color is not destroyed, we very well know . . . Notwithstanding the late diminution, it exists in many of our hotels: some of them would as soon

admit the dog from his kennel, at table, as the colored man; nevertheless, he is sought as a waiter; allowed to prepare their choicest dishes, and permitted to serve the white man, who would sneer and scorn to eat beside him. Prejudice is found also, in many of our schools,—even in those to which colored children are admitted; there is so much distinction made by prejudice, that the poor, timid colored children might about as well stay at home, as go to a school where they feel that they are looked upon as inferior, however much they may try to excel.

Nor is that hateful prejudice—so injurious to the soul, and all the best interests of the Negro—excluded from the professed church of Christ. Oh, no; we often find it in the house of worship, in all its cruel rigor. Where people assemble to worship a pure and holy God, who can look upon no sin with allowance . . . we often see the lip of some professed saint, curled in a scorn at a dusky face, or a scowl of disapprobation if a colored person sits elsewhere than by the door or on the stairs. How long, O Lord, must these things be!

The following selection is from the first two chapters of his book, depicting plantation life, the different conditions and positions of house slaves and field slaves, the fear of resistance among the plantation-owners, and the calculated methods of brutality used by the owners to hold the slaves down.

Slave Life on the Plantation

I was born in Prince William County, Virginia. At seven years of age, I found myself a slave on the plantation of Capt. William Helm. Our family consisted of my father and mother —whose names were Robert and Susan Steward—a sister, Mary, and myself. As was the usual custom, we lived in a small cabin, built of rough boards, with a floor of earth, and small openings in the sides of the cabin were substituted for windows. The chimney was built of sticks and mud; the door, of rough boards; and the whole was put together in the rudest possible manner. As to the furniture of this rude dwelling, it was procured by the slaves themselves, who were occasionally permitted to earn a little money after their day's toil was done. I never knew Capt. H. to furnish his slaves with household utensils of any description.

The amount of provision given out on the plantation per week, was invariably one peck of corn or meal for each slave. This allowance was given in meal when it could be obtained; when it could not, they received corn, which they pounded in mortars after they returned from their labor in the field. The slaves on our plantation were provided with very little meat. In addition to the peck of corn or meal, they were allowed a little salt and a few herrings. If they wished for more, they were obliged to earn it by over-work. They were permitted to cultivate small gardens, and were thereby enabled to provide themselves with many trifling conveniences. But these gardens were only allowed to some of the more industrious. Capt. Helm allowed his slaves a small quantity of meat during harvest time, but when the harvest was over they were obliged to fall back on the old allowance.

It was usual for men and women to work side by side on our plantation; and in many kinds of work, the women were compelled to do as much as the men. Capt. H. employed an overseer, whose business it was to look after each slave in the field, and see that he performed his task. The overseer always went around with a whip, about nine feet long, made of the toughest kind of cowhide, the butt-end of which was loaded with lead, and was about four or five inches in circumference, running to a point at the opposite extremity. This made a dreadful instrument of torture, and, when in the hands of a cruel overseer, it was truly fearful. With it, the skin of an ox or a horse could be cut through. Hence, it was no uncommon thing to see the poor slaves with their backs mangled in a most horrible manner. Our overseer, thus armed with his cowhide, and with a large bull-dog behind him, followed the slaves all day; and, if one of them fell in the rear from any cause, this cruel weapon was plied with terrible force. He would strike the dog one blow and the slave another, in order to keep the former from tearing the delinquent slave in pieces —such was the ferocity of his canine attendant.

It was the rule for the slaves to rise and be ready for their task by sun-rise, on the blowing of a horn or conch-shell; and woe be to the unfortunate, who was not in the field at the time appointed, which was in thirty minutes from the first sounding of the horn. I have heard the poor creatures beg as for their lives, of the inhuman overseer, to desist from his cruel punishment. Hence, they were usually found in the field "betimes in the morning," (to use an old Virginia phrase), where they worked until nine o'clock. They were then allowed thirty minutes to eat their morning meal, which consisted of a little bread. At a given signal, all hands were compelled to return to their work. They toiled until noon, when they were permitted to take their breakfast, which corresponds to our dinner.

On our plantation, it was the usual practice to have one of the old slaves set apart to do the cooking. All the field hands were required to give into the hands of the cook a certain portion of their weekly allowance, either in dough or meal, which was prepared in the following manner. The cook made a hot fire and rolled up each person's portion in some cabbage leaves, when they could be obtained, and placed it in a hole in the ashes, carefully covered with the same, where it remained until done. Bread baked in this way is very sweet and good. But cabbage leaves could not always be obtained. When this was the case, the bread was little better than a mixture of dough and ashes, which was not very palatable. The time allowed for breakfast, was one hour. At the signal, all hands were obliged to resume their toil. The overseer was always on hand to attend to all delinquents, who never failed to feel the blows of his heavy whip.

The usual mode of punishing the poor slaves was, to make them take off their clothes to the bare back, and then tie their hands before them with a rope, pass the end of the rope over a beam, and draw them up till they stood on the tips of their toes. Sometimes they tied their legs together and placed a rail between. Thus prepared, the overseer proceeded to punish the poor, helpless victim. Thirty-nine was the number of lashes ordinarily inflicted for the most trifling offence.

Who can imagine a position more painful? Oh, who, with feelings of common humanity, could look quietly on such torture? Who could remain unmoved, to see a fellow-creature thus tied, unable to move or to raise a hand in his own defence; scourged on his bare back, with a cowhide, until the blood flows in streams from his quivering flesh? And for what? Often for the most trifling fault; and, as sometimes occurs, because a mere whim or caprice of his brutal overseer demands it. Pale with passion, his eyes flashing and his stalwart frame trembling with rage, like some volcano, just ready to belch forth its fiery contents, and, in all its might and fury, spread death and destruction all around, he continues to wield the bloody lash on the broken flesh of the poor, pleading slave, until his arm grows weary, or he sinks down, utterly exhausted, on the very spot where already stand the pools of blood which his cruelty has drawn from the mangled body of his helpless victim, and within the hearing of those agonized groans and feeble cries of "Oh do, Massa! Oh do, Massa! Do, Lord, have mercy! Oh, Lord, have mercy!" &c.

Nor is this cruel punishment inflicted on the bare backs of the male portion of slaves only. Oh no! The slave husband must submit without a murmur, to see the form of his cherished, but wretched wife, not only exposed to the rude gaze of a beastly tyrant, but he must unresistingly see the heavy cowhide descend upon her shrinking flesh, and her manacled limbs writhe in inexpressible torture, while her piteous cries for help ring through his ears unanswered. The wild throbbing of his heart must be suppressed, and his righteous indignation find no voice, in the presence of the human monster who holds dominion over him.

After the infuriated and heartless overseer had satiated his thirst for vengeance, on the disobedient or delinquent slave, he was untied, and left to crawl away as best he could; sometimes on his hands and knees, to his lonely and dilapidated cabin, where, stretched upon the cold earth, he lay weak and bleeding and often faint from the loss of blood, without a friend who dare administer to his necessities, and groaning in the agony of his crushed spirit. In his cabin, which was not as good as many of our stables at the North, he might lie for weeks before recovering sufficient strength to resume the labor imposed upon him, and all this time without a bed or bed clothing, or any of the necessaries considered so essential to the sick.

Perhaps some of his fellow-slaves might come and bathe his wounds in warm water, to prevent his clothing from tearing open his flesh anew, and thus make the second suffering well nigh equal to the first; or they might from their scanty store bring him such food as they could spare, to keep him from suffering hunger, and offer their sympathy, and then drag their own weary bodies to their place of rest, after their daily task was finished. . . .

I once had the misfortune to break the lock of master's shot gun, and when it came to his knowledge, he came to me in a towering passion, and charged me with what he considered the *crime* of carelessness. I denied it, and told him I knew nothing about it; but I was so terribly frightened that he saw I was guilty, and told me so, foaming with rage; and then I confessed the truth. But oh, there was no escaping the lash. Its recollection is still bitter, and ever will be. I was commanded to take off my clothes, which I did, and then master put me on the back of another slave, my arms hanging down before him and my hands clasped in his, where he was obliged to hold me with a viselike grasp. Then master gave me the most severe flogging that I ever received, and I pray God that I may never again experience such torture. And yet Capt. Helm was not the worst of masters.

These cruelties are daily occurrences, and so degrading is the whole practice of Slavery, that it not only crushes and brutalizes the wretched slave, but it hardens the heart, benumbs all the fine feelings of humanity, and deteriorates from the character of the slaveholders themselves,—whether man or woman. Otherwise, how could a gentle, and in other respects, amiable woman, look on such scenes of cruelty, without a shudder of utter abhorrence? But slaveholding ladies, can not only look on quietly, but with approbation; and what is worse, though very common, they can and do use the lash and cowhide themselves, on the backs of their slaves, and that too on those of their own sex! Far rather would I spend my life in a State's Prison, than be the slave of the best slaveholder on the earth.

When I was not employed as an errand-boy, it was my duty to stand behind my master's chair, which was sometimes the whole day, never being allowed to sit in his presence. Indeed, no slave is ever allowed to sit down in the presence of their master or mistress. If a slave is addressed when sitting, he is required to spring to his feet, and instantly remove his hat, if he has one, and answer in the most humble manner, or lay the foundation for a flogging, which will not be long delayed.

I slept in the same room with my master and mistress. This room was elegantly furnished with damask curtains, mahogany bedstead of the most expensive kind, and every thing else about it was of the most costly kind. And while Mr. and Mrs. Helm reposed on their bed of down, with a cloud of lace floating over them, like some Eastern Prince, with their slaves to fan them while they slept, and to tremble when they awoke, I always slept upon the floor, without a pillow or even a blanket, but, like a dog, lay down anywhere I could find a place.

Slaves are never allowed to leave the plantation to which they belong, without a written pass. Should any one venture to disobey this law, he will most likely be caught by the *patrol* and given thirty-nine lashes. This patrol is always on duty every Sunday, going to each plantation under their supervision, entering every slave cabin, and examining closely the conduct of the slaves; and if they find one slave from another plantation without a pass, he is immediately punished with a severe flogging.

I recollect going one Sunday with my mother, to visit my grand-mother; and while there, two or three of the patrol came and looked into the cabin, and seeing my mother, demanded her pass. She told them that she had one, but had left it in another cabin, from whence she soon brought it, which saved her a whipping but we were terribly frightened.

The reader will obtain a better knowledge of the character of a Virginia patrol, by the relation of an affair, which came off on the neighboring plantation of Col. Alexander, in which some forty of Capt. Helm's slaves were engaged, and which proved rather destructive of human life in the end.

But I must first say that it is not true, that slave owners are respected for kindness to their slaves. The more tyrannical a master is, the more will he be favorably regarded by his neighboring planters; and from the day that he acquires the reputation of a kind and indulgent master, he is looked upon with suspicion, and sometimes hatred, and his slaves are watched more closely than before.

Col. Alexander was a very wealthy planter and owned a great number of slaves, but he was very justly suspected of being a kind, humane, and indulgent master. His slaves were

7 Slave revolts were a prominent part of the history of slavery,
including those aboard ships. In the famous revolt aboard the Spanish
ship *Amistad* in 1839, shown in this engraving, the slaves took over

the ship off the coast of Cuba, sailed it to Montauk, Long Island, and won their freedom in a long legal battle ultimately decided by the American Supreme Court

always better fed, better clad, and had greater privileges than any I knew in the Old Dominion; and of course, the patrol had long had an eye on them, anxious to flog some of "those pampered niggers, who were spoiled by the indulgence of a weak, inefficient, but well-meaning owner."

Col. A. gave his slaves the liberty to get up a grand dance. Invitations were sent and accepted, to a large number of slaves on other plantations, and so, for miles around, all or many of the slaves were in high anticipation of joining in the great dance, which was to come off on Easter night. In the mean time, the patrol was closely watching their movements, and evinced rather a joyful expectancy of the many they should find there without a pass, and the flogging they would give them for that, if not guilty of any other offence, and perhaps they might catch some of the Colonel's slaves doing something for which they could be taught "to know their place," by the application of the cowhide.

The slaves of Col. A.'s plantation had to provide and prepare the supper for the expected vast "turn out," which was no light matter; and as slaves like on such occasions to pattern as much as possible after their master's family, the result was, to meet the emergency of the case, they *took,* without saying, "by your leave, Sir," some property belonging to their master, reasoning among themselves, as slaves often do, that it can not be *stealing,* because "it belongs to massa, and so do *we,* and we only use one part of his property to benefit another. Sure, 'tis all massa's." And if they do not get detected in this removal of "massa's property" from one location to another, they think no more of it.

Col. Alexander's slaves were hurrying on with their great preparations for the dance and feast; and as the time drew near, the old and knowing ones might be seen in groups, discussing the matter, with many a wink and nod; but it was in the valleys and by-places where the younger portion were to be found, rather secretly preparing food for the great time coming. This consisted of hogs, sheep, calves; and as to master's *poultry,* that suffered daily. Sometimes it was missed, but the disappearance was always easily accounted for, by informing "massa" that a great number of hawks had been around of late; and their preparation went on, night after night, undetected. They who repaired to a swamp or other by-place to cook by night, carefully destroyed everything likely to detect them, before they returned to their cabins in the morning.

The night for the dance *came* at last, and long before the time, the road leading to Col. Alexander's plantation presented a gay spectacle. The females were seen flocking to the place of resort, with heads adorned with gaudy bandanna turbans and new calico dresses, of the gayest colors,—their whole attire decked over with bits of gauze ribbon and other fantastic finery. The shades of night soon closed over the plantation, and then could be heard the rude music and loud laugh of the unpolished slave. It was about ten o'clock when the *aristocratic slaves* began to assemble, dressed in the cast-off finery of their master and mistress, swelling out and putting on airs in imitation of those they were forced to obey from day to day.

When they were all assembled, the dance commenced; the old fiddler struck up some favorite tune, and over the floor they went; the flying feet of the dancers were heard, pat, pat, over the apartment till the clock warned them it was twelve at midnight, or what some call "low twelve," to distinguish it from twelve o'clock at noon; then the violin ceased its discordant sounds, and the merry dancers paused to take breath.

Supper was then announced, and all began to prepare for the sumptuous feast. It being the pride of slaves to imitate the manners of their master and mistress, especially in the ceremonies of the table, all was conducted with great propriety and good order. The food was well cooked, and in a very plentiful supply. They had also managed in some way, to get a good quantity of excellent wine, which was sipped in the most approved and modern style. Every dusky face was lighted up, and every eye sparkled with joy. However ill-fed they might have been, here, for once, there was plenty. Suffering and toil was forgotten, and they all seemed with one accord to give themselves up to the intoxication of pleasurable amusement.

House servants were of course, "the stars" of the party; all eyes were turned to them to see how they conducted, for they, among slaves, are what a military man would call "fuglemen." The field hands, and such of them as have generally been excluded from the dwelling of their owners, look to the house servant as a pattern of politeness and gentility. And indeed, it is often the only method of obtaining any knowledge of the manners of what is called "genteel society"; hence, they are ever regarded as a privileged class; and are sometimes greatly envied, while others are bitterly hated. And too often justly, for many of them are the most despicable talebearers and mischief-makers, who will, for the sake of the favor of his master or mistress, frequently betray his fellow-slave, and by tattling, get him severely whipped; and for these acts of perfidy, and sometimes downright falsehood, he is often rewarded by his master, who knows it is for his interest to keep such ones about him; though he is sometimes obliged, in addition to a reward, to send him away, for fear of the vengeance of the betrayed slaves. In the family of his master, the example of bribery and treachery is ever set before him, hence it is, that insurrections and stampedes are so generally detected. Such slaves are always treated with more affability than others; for the slaveholder is well aware that he stands over a volcano, that may at any moment rock his foundation to the center, and with one mighty burst of its long suppressed fire, sweep him and his family to destruction. When he lies down at night, he knows not but that ere another morning shall dawn, he may be left mangled and bleeding, and at the mercy of those maddened slaves whom he has so long ruled with a rod of iron.

But the supper, like other events, came to an end at last. The expensive table service, with other things, which had been secretly brought from the "great house," was hurriedly cleansed by the slaves, and carefully returned. The floor was again cleared, the violin sounded, and soon they were performing another "break down," with all the wild abandon of the African character,—in the very midst of which, the music suddenly ceased, and the old musician assumed a listening attitude. Every foot was motionless; every face terrified, and every ear listening for the cause of the alarm.

Soon the slave who was kept on the "look-out," shouted to the listeners the single word *"patrol!"* and then the tumult that followed that announcement, is beyond the power of language to describe! Many a poor slave who had stolen from his cabin, to join in the dance, now remembered that they had no pass! Many screamed in affright, as if they already felt the lash and heard the crack of the overseer's whip; others clenched their hands, and assumed an attitude of bold defiance, while a savage frown contracted the brow of all. Their unrestrained merriment and delicious fare seemed to arouse in them the natural feelings of self-defence and defiance of their oppressors. But what could be done? The patrol was nearing the building, when an athletic, powerful slave, who had been but a short time from his "fatherland," whose spirit the cowardly overseer had labored in vain to quell, said in a calm, clear voice, that we had better stand our ground, and advised the females to lose no time in useless wailing, but get their things and repair immediately to a cabin at a short distance, and there remain quiet, without a light, which they did with all possible haste. The men were terrified at this bold act of their leader; and many with dismay at the thought of resistance, began to skulk behind fences and old buildings, when he opened the door and requested every slave to leave

8 On arrival in the United States the cargoes of the slave ships were taken to markets like this one in the port city of New Orleans

who felt unwilling to fight. None were urged to remain, and those who stood by him did so voluntarily.

Their number was now reduced to twenty-five men, but the leader, a gigantic African, with a massive, compact frame, and an arm of great strength, looked competent to put ten common men to flight. He clenched his powerful fist, and declared that he would resist unto death, before he would be arrested by those savage men, even if they promised not to flog him. They closed the door, and agreed not to open it; and then the leader cried; "Extinguish the lights and let them come! we will meet them hand to hand!" Five of the number he stationed near the door, with orders to rush out, if the patrol entered, and seize their horses, cut the bridles, or otherwise unfit them for use. This would prevent them from giving an alarm and getting a reinforcement from surrounding plantations. In silence they awaited the approach of the enemy, and soon the tramping of horses' feet announced their approach, but when within a few yards of the house they halted, and were overheard by one of the skulking slaves, maturing their plans and mode of attack. There was great hesitancy expressed by a part of the company to engage in the affair at all.

"Coming events cast their shadow before."

The majority, however, seemed to think it safe enough, and uttered expressions of triumph that they had got the rascals at last.

"Are you not afraid that they will resist?" said the weaker party.

"Resist?" was the astonished answer. "This old fellow, the Colonel, has pampered and indulged his slaves, it is true, and they have slipped through our fingers whenever we have attempted to chastise them; but they are not such fools as to dare resistance! Those niggers know as well as we, that it is *death*, by the law of the State, for a slave to strike a white man."

"Very true," said the other, "but it is dark and long past midnight, and beside they have been indulging their appetites, and we cannot tell what they may attempt to do."

"Pshaw!" he answered, contemptuously, "they are unarmed, and I should not fear in the least, to go in among them *alone,* armed only with my cowhide!"

"As you please, then," he said, rather dubiously, "but look well to your weapons; are they in order?"

"In prime order, Sir." And putting spurs to their horses, were soon at the house, where they dismounted and requested one of the party to remain with the horses.

"What," said he, "are you so chicken-hearted as to suppose those d——d cowardly niggers are going to get up an insurrection?"

"Oh no," he replied, carelessly, but would not consent to have the horses left alone. "Besides," said he, "they may forget themselves at this late hour; but if they do, a few lashes of the cowhide will quicken their memory, I reckon."

The slaves were aware of their movements, and prepared to receive them.

They stepped up to the door boldly, and demanded admittance, but all was silent; they tried to open it, but it was fastened. Those inside, ranged on each side of the door, and stood perfectly still.

The patrol finding the slaves not disposed to obey, burst off the slight fastening that secured the door, and the chief of the patrol bounded into their midst, followed by several of his companions, all in total darkness!

Vain is the attempt to describe the tumultuous scene which followed. Hand to hand they fought and struggled with each other, amid the terrific explosion of firearms,—oaths and curses, mingled with the prayers of the wounded, and the groans of the dying! Two of the patrol were killed on the spot, and lay drenched in the warm blood that so lately flowed through their veins. Another with his arm broken and otherwise wounded, lay groaning and helpless, beside the fallen slaves, who had sold their lives so dearly. Another of his fellows was found at a short distance, mortally wounded and about to bid adieu to life. In the yard lay the keeper of the horses, a stiffened corpse. Six of the slaves were killed and two wounded.

It would be impossible to convey to the minds of northern people, the alarm and perfect consternation that the above circumstances occasioned in that community. The knowledge of its occurrence was carried from one plantation to another, as on the wings of the wind; exaggerated accounts were given, and prophecies of the probable result made, until the excitement became truly fearful. Every cheek was blanched and every frame trembled when listening to the tale, that "insurrection among the slaves had commenced on the plantation of Col. Alexander; that three or four of the patrol had been killed, &c." The day after, people flocked from every quarter, armed to the teeth, swearing vengence on the defenceless slaves. Nothing can teach plainer than this, the constant and tormenting fear in which the slaveholder lives, and yet he repents not of his deeds.

Slaves did not only live on plantations. By 1820, 37 per cent of the inhabitants in the towns of the South were Blacks, and at one time the number of urban slaves, working in factories and shops and other urban occupations, was as high as 22 per cent of all of the slaves in the South. In 1850 there were 400,000 slaves living in urban communities. By 1860, the eve of the Civil War, the proportion of slaves in the towns had dropped considerably, even though the number of slaves in the South as a whole had risen, because the slave-owning forces became convinced that the towns were not good places to maintain their control and domination. The plantation system of subjugation and brutalized control could not operate as effectively in the towns. Slaves in the towns had free time and could meet with other slaves and with people and conditions of all kinds. Some could find ingenious ways to learn to read and write, in defiance of the anti-literacy laws in the South, and others found ways of escape, having obtained skills and occupations they could well use as free men. In the following little-known narrative, which was dictated by the author to a friend after his escape from slavery, and was published in Canada in 1853, we are told the story of the life of one slave who worked in a small shop and how he was able to become literate.

How I Learned to Read and Write

I was born a slave. My recollections of early life are associated with poverty, suffering and shame. I was made to feel, in my boyhood's first experience, that I was inferior and degraded, and that I must pass through life in a dependent and suffering condition. The experience of forty-three years, which were passed by me in slavery, was one of dark fears and darker realities. . . . I remember well that dear old cabin, with its clay floor and mud chimney, in which, for nine years, I enjoyed the presence and love of my wretched parents.

Father and mother tried to make it a happy place for their dear children. *They* worked late into the night many and many a time to get a little simple furniture for their home and the home of their children; and they spent many hours of willing toil to stop up the chinks between the logs of their poor hut, that they and their children might be protected from the storm and the cold. I can testify, from my own painful experience, to the deep and fond affection which the slave cherishes in his heart for his home and its dear ones. . . .

My mistress complained of me at length, that I was not so obedient as I ought to be, and so I was taken from the house into the store. My business there was to open and sweep out the store in the morning, and get all the things ready for the accommodation of customers who might come in during the day. Then I had to bring out and deliver all heavy articles that might be called for during the day, such as salt, large quantities of which were sold in the store; ship stores, grain, &c., &c. . . .

After my master dismissed Mr. C., he tried to get along with me alone in the store. He kept the books and waited upon the most genteel of his customers, leaving me to do the rest of the work. This went on six months, when he declared that he could not bear this confinement any longer; and so he got a white boy to come and enter as clerk, to stay till he was of age. James Dixon was a poor boy, about my own age, and when he came into the store, could hardly read or write. He was accordingly engaged a part of each day with his books and writing. I saw him studying, and asked him to let me see his book. When he felt in a good humor, James was very kind and obliging. The great trouble with him was, that his fits of ill-humor were much more frequent than his times of good feeling. It happened, however, that he was on good terms with himself when I asked him to show me his book, and so he let me take it, and look at it, and he answered very kindly many questions which I asked him about books and schools and learning. He told me that he was trying to get learning enough to fit him to do a good business for himself after he should get through with Mr. Jones. He told me that a man who had learning would always find friends, and get along very well in the world without having to work hard, while those who had no learning would have no friends and be compelled to work very hard for a poor living all their days. This was all new to me, and furnished me topics for wondering thought for days afterwards. The result of my meditations was, that an intense burning desire to learn to read and write took possession of my mind, occupying me wholly in waking hours, and stirring up earnest thoughts in my soul even when I slept. The question, which then took hold of my whole consciousness was, how can I get a book to begin? James told me that a spelling-book was the first one necessary in getting learning. So I contrived how I might obtain a spelling-book. At length, after much study, I hit upon this plan: I cleaned the boots of a Mr. David Smith, Jr., who carried on the printing business, in Wilmington, and edited the Cape Fear Recorder. He had always appeared to me to be a very kind man. I thought I would get him to aid me in procuring a spelling-book. So I went one morning, with a beating heart, into his office, and asked him to sell me a spelling-book. He looked at me in silence, and with close attention, for some time, and asked me what I wanted. I told him I wanted to learn to read. He shook his head, and replied, "No, Thomas, it would not answer for me to sell you a book to learn out of; *you* must not learn to read; you will only get yourself into trouble if you attempt it;

and I advise you to get that foolish notion out of your head as quickly as you can."

David's brother, Peter Smith, kept a book and stationery store under the printing office, and I next applied to him for a book, determined to persevere till I obtained this coveted treasure. He asked me the same question that his brother David had done, and with the same searching, suspicious look. By my previous repulse I had discovered that I could not get a spelling-book if I told what I wanted to do with it, and so I told a lie, in order to get it. I answered, that I wanted it for a white boy, naming one that lived at my master's, and that he had given me the money to get it with, and had asked me to call at the store and buy it. The book was then handed out to me, the money taken in return, and I left, feeling very rich with my long desired treasure. I got out of the store, and, looking round to see that no one observed me, I hid my book in my bosom, and hurried on to my work, conscious that a new era in my life was opening upon me through the possession of this book. That consciousness at once awakened new thoughts, purposes, and hopes, a new life, in fact, in my experience. My mind was excited. The words spoken by James Dixon of the great advantages of learning, made me intensely anxious to learn. I was a slave; and I knew that the whole community was in league to keep the poor slave in ignorance and chains. Yet I longed to be free, and to be able to move the minds of other men by my thoughts. It seemed to me now, that, if I could learn to read and write, this learning might—nay, I really thought it would, point out to me the way to freedom, influence, and real, secure happiness. So I hurried on to my master's store, and, watching my opportunity to do it safe from curious eyes, I hid my book with the utmost care, under some liquor barrels in the smoke house. The first opportunity I improved to examine my book. I looked it over with the most intent eagerness, turned over its leaves, and tried to discover what the new and strange characters which I saw in its pages might mean. But I found it a vain endeavour. I could understand a picture, and from it make out a story of immediate interest to my mind. But I could not associate any thought or fact with these crooked letters with which my primer was filled. So the next day I sought a favorable moment, and asked James to tell me where a scholar must begin in order to learn to read, and how. He laughed at my ignorance, and, taking his spelling-book, showed me the alphabet in large and small letters on the same page. I asked him the name of the first letter, pointing it out, he told me A; so of the next, and so on through the alphabet. I managed to remember A and B, and I studied and looked out the same letters in many other parts of the book. And so I fixed in a tenacious memory the names of the two first letters of the alphabet. But I found I could not get on without help, and so I applied to James again to show me the letters and tell me their names. This time he suspected me of trying to learn to read myself, and he plied me with questions till he ascertained that I was, in good earnest, entering upon an effort to get knowledge. At this discovery, he manifested a good deal of indignation. He told me, in scorn, that it was not for such as *me* to try to improve, that *I* was a *slave,* and that it was not proper for *me* to learn to read. He threatened to tell my master, and at length, by his hard language, my anger was fully aroused, and I answered taunt with taunt. He called me a poor, miserable nigger; and I called him a poor, ignorant white servant boy. While we were engaged in loud and angry words, of mutual defiance and scorn, my master came into the store. Mr. Jones had never given me a whipping since the time I have already described, during my first year of toil, want and suffering in his service. But he had now caught me in the unpardonable offense of giving saucy language to a white boy, and one, too, who was in his employ. Without stopping to make any enquiries, he took down the cowhide, and gave me a severe whipping. He told me never to talk

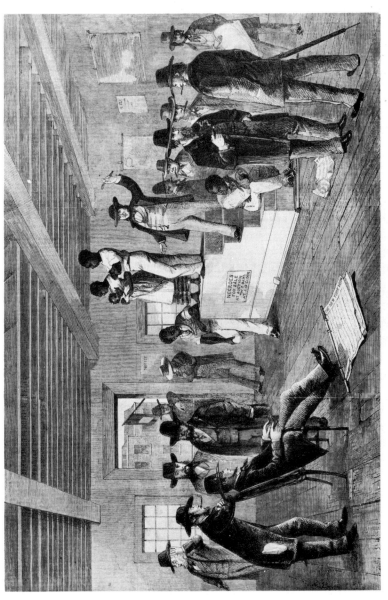

9 On the auction block. "How much, gentlemen, how much? Bid up, bid up, gentle-men, they must be sold," cries the auctioneer, as the runaway Peter Randolph described in his narrative *Sketches of Slave Life*

back to a white man on pain of flogging. I suppose this law or custom is universal at the south. And I suppose it is thought necessary to enforce this habit of obsequious submission on the part of the colored people to the whites, in order to maintain their supremacy over the poor, outraged slaves.

I will mention, in this connection, as illustrative of this cruel custom, an incident which I saw just before I ran away from my chains. A little colored boy was carrying along through Wilmington a basket of food. His name was Ben, and he belonged to Mrs. Runkin, a widow lady. A little mischievous white boy, just about Ben's age and size, met him, and purposely overturned the little fellow's basket, and scattered his load in the mud. Ben, in return for this wanton act, called him some hard name, when the white boy clinched him to throw him down with the scattered fragments upon his basket in the mud. Ben resisted, and threw down the white boy, proving to be the stronger of the two. Tom Myers, a young lawyer of Wilmington, saw the contest, and immediately rushing out, seized little Ben, and dragged him into the store opposite the place of battle. He sent out to a saddler's shop, procured a cow-hide, and gave this little fellow a tremendous flogging, for the daring crime of resisting a white boy who had wantonly invaded his rights. Is it any wonder that the spirit of self-respect of the poor, ignorant slave is broken down by such treatment of unsparing and persevering cruelty?

I was now repulsed by James, so that I could hope for no assistance from him in learning to read. But I could not go on alone. I must get some one to aid me in starting, or give up the effort to learn. This I could not bear to do. I longed to be able to read, and so I cast about me to see what I should do next. I thought of a kind boy at the bake-house, near my own age. I thought he would help me, and so I went to him, showed my book, and asked him to teach me the letters. He told their names, and went over the whole alphabet with me three times. By this assistance, I learned a few more of the letters, so that I could remember them afterwards when I sat down alone and tried to call them over. I could now pick out and name five or six of the letters in any part of the book. I felt then that I was getting along, and the consciousness that I was making progress, though slow and painful, was joy and hope to my sorrowing heart, such as I had never felt before. I could not with safety go to the bake-house, as there I was exposed to detection by the sudden entrance of customers or idlers. I wanted to get a teacher who would give me a little aid each day, and now I set about securing this object. As kind Providence would have it, I easily succeeded, and on this wise: A little boy, Hiram Bricket, ten years old, or about that age, came along by the store one day, on his way home from school, while my master was gone home to dinner, and James was in the front part of the store. I beckoned to Hiram to come round to the back door; and with him I made a bargain to meet me each day at noon, when I was allowed a little while to get my dinner, and to give me instruction in reading. I was to give him six cents a week. I met him the next day at his father's stable, the place agreed upon for our daily meeting; and, going into one of the stables, the noble little Hiram gave me a thorough lesson in the alphabet. I learned it nearly all at that time, with what study I could give it by stealth during the day and night. And then again I felt lifted up and happy.

I was permitted to enjoy these advantages, however, but a short time. A black boy, belonging to Hiram's father, one day discovered our meeting and what we were doing. He told his master of it, and Hiram was at once forbidden this employment. I had then got along so that I was reading and spelling in words of two syllables. My noble little teacher was very patient and faithful with me, and my days were passing away in very great happiness under the consciousness that I was learning to read. I felt at night, as I went to my rest, that I was really beginning to be a *man,* preparing myself for a condition in life better and higher, and happier than could belong to the ignorant *slave.* And in this blessed feeling I found, waking and sleeping, a most precious happiness.

After I was deprived of my kind little teacher, I plodded on the best way I could by myself, and in this way I got into words of five syllables. I got some little time to study by daylight in the morning, before any of my master's family had risen. I got a moment's opportunity also at noon, and sometimes at night. During the day, I was in the back store a good deal, and whenever I thought I could have five minutes to myself, I would take my book and try to learn a little in reading and spelling. If I heard James, or master Jones, or any customer coming in, I would drop my book among the barrels, and pretend to be very busy shovelling the salt or doing some other work. Several times I came very near being detected. My master suspected something, because I was so still in the back room, and a number of times he came very slyly to see what I was about. But at such times I was always so fortunate as to hear his tread or see his shadow on the wall in time to hide away my book.

When I had got along to words of five syllables, I went to see a colored friend, Ned Cowan, whom I knew I could trust. I told him I was trying to learn to read, and asked him to help me a little. He said he did not dare to give me any instruction, but he heard me read a few words, and then told me I should learn if I would only persevere as nobly as I had done thus far. I told him *how* I had got along, and what difficulties I had met with. He encouraged me, and spoke very kindly of my efforts to improve my condition by getting learning. He told me I had got along far enough to get another book, in which I could learn to write the letters, as well as to read. He told me where and how to procure this book. I followed his directions, and obtained another spelling-book at Worcester's store, in Wilmington. Jacob showed me a little about writing. He set me a copy, first of straight marks. I now got me a box which I could hide under my bed, some ink, pens, and a bit of candle. So, when I went to bed, I pulled my box out from under my cot, turned it up on end, and began my first attempt at writing. I worked away till my candle was burned out, and then laid down to sleep. Jacob next set me a copy, which he called pothooks; then, the letters of the alphabet. These letters were also in my spelling-book, and according to Jacob's directions, I set them before me for a copy, and wrote on these exercises till I could form all the letters and call them by name. One evening I wrote out my name in large letters—THOMAS JONES. This I carried to Jacob, in a great excitement of happiness. . . .

WILLIAM WELLS BROWN

The most prolific and versatile of the Afro-American writers of the nineteenth century, William Wells Brown published his first autobiographical slave narrative in 1847 and went on to write the first novel, the first play, and the first travel book by an American Black man, as well as many other books. The full text of his illuminating *The Narrative of William W. Brown, a Fugitive Slave* is currently available in a number of reprint editions of slave narratives. For this collection I have selected a sketch of slave life from a later, lesser-known, and not easily accessible book by Brown, *My Southern Home: Or, the South and Its People*, first published in Boston in 1880. The book consists of recollections of slave life in the South, as well as later sketches based on visits there. The following story of slave life, Chapter VII in the book, is entitled "The Goopher King". Because current dictionaries do not always define the word "goopher" in the sense in which Brown used it, a word of explanation may be in place. "Goopher" is not a variant of "goofy" or "goofiness" in its modern slang sense. "The Goopher King" is a master conjure man, a man with magic powers to summon the devil or spirits, to cast spells, and to perform miracles.

The Goopher King

Forty years ago, in the Southern States, superstition held an exalted place with all classes, but more especially with the blacks and uneducated, or poor, whites. This was shown more clearly in their belief in witchcraft in general, and the devil in particular. To both of these classes, the devil was a real

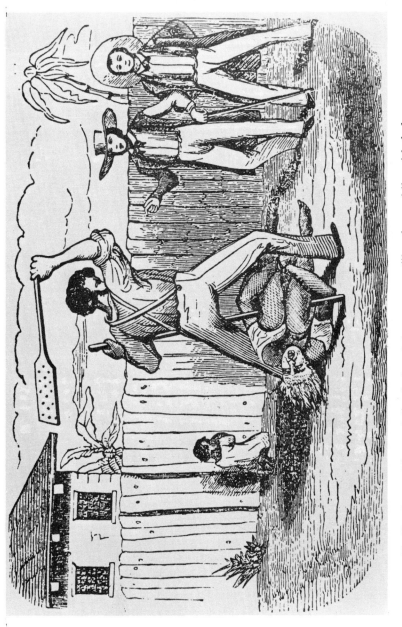

10 Beatings with specially designed instruments, like the paddle with holes seen here, and other forms of torture were used to control and subjugate the slaves

being, sporting a club-foot, horns, tail, and a hump on his back.

The influence of the devil was far greater than that of the Lord. If one of these votaries had stolen a pig, and the fear of the Lord came over him, he would most likely ask the Lord to forgive him, but still cling to the pig. But if the fear of the devil came upon him, in all probability he would drop the pig and take to his heels.

In those days the city of St. Louis had a large number who had implicit faith in Voudooism. I once attended one of their midnight meetings. In the pale rays of the moon the dark outlines of a large assemblage was visible, gathered about a small fire, conversing in different tongues. They were negroes of all ages,—women, children, and men. Finally, the noise was hushed, and the assembled group assumed an attitude of respect. They made way for their queen, and a short, black, old negress came upon the scene, followed by two assistants, one of whom bore a cauldron, and the other, a box.

The cauldron was placed over the dying embers, the queen drew forth, from the folds of her gown, a magic wand, and the crowd formed a ring around her. Her first act was to throw some substance on the fire, the flames shot up with a lurid glare—now it writhed in serpent coils, now it darted upward in forked tongues, and then it gradually transformed itself into a veil of dusky vapors. At this stage, after a certain amount of gibberish and wild gesticulation from the queen, the box was opened, and frogs, lizards, snakes, dog liver, and beef hearts drawn forth and thrown into the cauldron. Then followed more gibberish and gesticulation, when the congregation joined hands, and began the wildest dance imaginable, keeping it up until the men and women sank to the ground from mere exhaustion.

In the ignorant days of slavery, there was a general belief that a horse-shoe hung over the door would insure good luck. I have seen negroes, otherwise comparatively intelligent, refuse to pick up a pin, needle, or other such object, dropped by a negro, because, as they alleged, if the person who dropped the articles had a spite against them, to touch anything they dropped would voudou them, and make them seriously ill.

Nearly every large plantation, with any considerable number of negroes, had at least one, who laid claim to be a fortune-teller, and who was regarded with more than common respect by his fellow-slaves. Dinkie, a full-blooded African, large in frame, coarse featured, and claiming to be a descendant of a king in his native land, was the oracle on the "Poplar Farm." At the time of which I write, Dinkie was about fifty years of age, and had lost an eye, and was, to say the least, a very ugly-looking man.

No one in that section was considered so deeply immersed in voudooism, goopherism, and fortune-telling, as he. Although he had been many years in the Gaines family, no one could remember the time when Dinkie was called upon to perform manual labor. He was not sick, yet he never worked. No one interfered with him. If he felt like feeding the chickens, pigs, or cattle, he did so. Dinkie hunted, slept, was at the table at meal time, roamed through the woods, went to the city, and returned when he pleased, with no one to object, or to ask a question. Everybody treated him with respect. The whites, throughout the neighborhood, tipped their hats to the old one-eyed negro, while the policemen, or patrollers, permitted him to pass without a challenge. The negroes, everywhere, stood in mortal fear of "Uncle Dinkie." The blacks who saw him every day, were always thrown upon their good behavior, when in his presence. I once asked a negro why they appeared to be afraid of Dinkie. He looked at me, shrugged his shoulders, smiled, shook his head and said,—

"I ain't afraid of de debble, but I ain't ready to go to him jess yet." He then took a look around and behind, as if he feared some one would hear what he was saying, and then continued: "Dinkie's got de power, ser; he knows things seen and unseen, an' dat's what makes him his own massa."

It was literally true, this man was his own master. He wore a snake's skin around his neck, carried a petrified frog in one pocket, and a dried lizard in the other.

A slave speculator once came along and offered to purchase Dinkie. Dr. Gaines, no doubt, thought it a good opportunity to get the elephant off his hands, and accepted the money. A day later, the trader returned the old negro, with a threat of a suit at law for damages.

A new overseer was employed, by Dr. Gaines, to take charge of "Poplar Farm." His name was Grove Cook, and he was widely known as a man of ability in managing plantations, and raising a large quantity of produce from a given number of hands. Cook was called a "hard overseer." The negroes dreaded his coming, and, for weeks before his arrival, the overseer's name was on every slave's tongue.

Cook came, he called the negroes up, men and women; counted them, looked them over as a purchaser would a drove of cattle that he intended to buy. As he was about to dismiss them he saw Dinkie come out his cabin. The sharp eye of the overseer was at once on him.

"Who is that nigger?" inquired Cook.

"That is Dinkie," replied Dr. Gaines.

"What is his place?" continued the overseer.

"Oh, Dinkie is a gentleman at large!" was the response.

"Have you any objection to his working?"

"None, whatever."

"Well, sir," said Cook, "I'll put him to work to-morrow morning."

Dinkie was called up and counted in.

At the roll call, the following morning, all answered except the conjurer; he was not there.

The overseer inquired for Dinkie, and was informed that he was still asleep.

"I will bring him out of his bed in a hurry," said Cook, as he started towards the negro's cabin. Dinkie appeared at his door, just as the overseer was approaching.

"Follow me to the barn," said the impatient driver to the negro. "I make it a point always to whip a nigger, the first day that I take charge of a farm, so as to let the hands know who I am. And, now, Mr. Dinkie, they tell me that you have not had your back tanned for many years; and, that being the case, I shall give you a flogging that you will never forget. Follow me to the barn." Cook started for the barn, but turned and went into his house to get his whip.

At this juncture, Dinkie gave a knowing look to the other slaves, who were standing by, and said, "Ef he lays the weight ob his fingers on me, you'll see de top of dat barn come off."

The reappearance of the overseer, with the large negro whip in one hand, and a club in the other, with the significant demand of "follow me," caused a deep feeling in the breast of every negro present.

Dr. Gaines, expecting a difficulty between his new driver and the conjurer, had arisen early, and was standing at his bedroom window looking on.

The news that Dinkie was to be whipped, spread far and near over the place, and had called forth men, women, and children. Even Uncle Ned, the old negro of ninety years, had crawled out of his straw, and was at his cabin door. As the barn doors closed behind the overseer and Dinkie, a death-like silence prevaded the entire group, who, instead of going to their labor, as ordered by the driver, were standing as if paralyzed, gazing intently at the barn, expecting every moment to see the roof lifted.

Not a word was spoken by anyone, except Uncle Ned, who smiled, shook his head, put on a knowing countenance, and said, "My word fer it, de oberseer ain't agwine to whip Dinkie."

Five minutes, ten minutes, fifteen minutes passed, and the usual sound of "Oh, pray, massa! Oh, pray, massa!" heard on the occasion of a slave being punished, had not yet proceeded from the barn.

Many of the older negroes gathered around Uncle Ned, for he and Dinkie occupied the same cabin, and the old, superannuated slave knew more about the affairs of the conjurer, than anyone else. Ned told of how, on the previous night, Dinkie had slept but little, had closely inspected the snake's skin around his neck, the petrified frog and dried lizard, in his pockets, and had rubbed himself all over with goopher; and when he had finished, he knelt, and exclaimed,—

"Now, good and lovely devil, for more than twenty years, I have served you faithfully. Before I got into your service, de white folks bought an' sold me an' my old wife an' chillen, an' whip me, and half starve me. Dey did treat me mighty bad, dat you knows. Den I use to pray to de Lord, but dat did no good, kase de white folks don't fear de Lord. But dey fears you, an' ever since I got into your service, I is able to do as I please. No white dares to lay his hand on me; and dis is all owing to de power dat you give me. Oh, good and lovely devil! please to continer dat power. A new oberseer is to come here to-morrow, an' he wants to get me in his hands. But, dear devil, I axe you to stand by me in dis my trial hour, an' I will neber desert you as long as I live. Continer dis power; make me strong in your cause; make me to be more faithful to you, an' let me still be able to conquer my enemies, an' I will give you all de glory, and will try to deserve a seat at your right hand."

With bated breath, everyone listened to Uncle Ned. All had the utmost confidence in Dinkie's "power." None believed that he would be punished, while a large number expected to see the roof of the barn burst off at any moment. At last the suspense was broken. The barn door flew open; the overseer and the conjurer came out together, walking side by side, and

1838.] SEPTEMBER—NINTH MONTH. [30 days.

Sometimes a slave is tied up, by the wrists, while the ancles are fastened to a staple in the floor. In this position, they are punished with the whip or with the paddle. This is an instrument of torture bored full of holes, each hole raising a blister.

11 Elaborate systems for whipping slaves are exposed in the *American Anti-Slavery Almanac for 1838*

separated when half-way up the walk. As they parted, Cook went to the field, and Dinkie to his cabin.

The slaves all shook their heads significantly. The fact that the old negro had received no punishment, was evidence of his victory over the slave driver. But how the feat had been accomplished, was a mystery. No one dared to ask Dinkie, for he was always silent, except when he had something to communicate. Everyone was afraid to inquire of the overseer.

There was, however, one faint chance of getting an inkling of what had occurred in the barn, and that was through Uncle Ned. This fact made the old, superannuated slave the hero and centre of attraction, for several days. Many were the applications made to Ned for information, but the old man did not know, or wished to exaggerate the importance of what he had learned.

"I tell you," said Dolly, "Dinkie is a power."

"He's nobody's fool," responded Hannah.

"I would not make him mad wid me, fer dis whole world," ejaculated Jim.

Just then, Nancy, the cook, came in brim full of news. She had given Uncle Ned some "cracklin bread," which had pleased the old man so much that he had opened his bosom, and told her all that he got from Dinkie. This piece of information flew quickly from cabin to cabin, and brought the slaves hastily into the kitchen.

It was night. Nancy sat down, looked around, and told Billy to shut the door. This heightened the interest, so that the fall of a pin could have been heard. All eyes were upon Nancy, and she felt keenly the importance of her position. Her voice was generally loud, with a sharp ring, which could be heard for a long distance, especially in the stillness of the night. But now, Nancy spoke in a whisper, occasionally putting her finger to her mouth, indicating a desire for silence, even when the breathing of those present could be distinctly heard.

"When dey got in de barn, de oberseer said to Dinkie, 'Strip yourself; I don't want to tear your clothes with my whip. I'm going to tear your black skin.'

"Den, you see, Dinkie tole de oberseer to look in de east corner ob de barn. He looked, an' he saw hell, wid all de torments, an' de debble, with his cloven foot, a-struttin' aboud dar, jes as ef he was cock ob de walk. An' Dinkie tole Cook, dat ef he lay his finger on him, he'd call de debble up to take him away."

"An' what did Cook say to dat?" asked Jim.

"Let me 'lone; I didn't tell you all," said Nancy. "Den you see de oberseer turn pale in de face, an' he say to Dinkie, 'Let me go dis time, an' I'll nebber trouble you any more.' "

This concluded Nancy's story, as related to her by old Ned, and religiously believed by all present. Whatever caused the overseer to change his mind in regard to the flogging of Dinkie, it was certain that he was most thoroughly satisfied to let the old negro off without the threatened punishment; and, although he remained at "Poplar Farm," as overseer, for five years, he never interfered with the conjurer again.

It is not strange that ignorant people should believe in characters of Dinkie's stamp; but it is really marvellous that well-educated men and women should give any countenance whatever, to such delusions as were practised by the oracle of "Poplar Farm."

In this story, and in others in this book, we encounter conflicts with the overseer, an important figure in all large plantations. The plantation system was developed and used in the cultivation of cotton and the staple crops of the deep South. But not all plantations were large. Actually the bulk of the plantations were owned by small farmers. In 1860, out of a total of 338,000 slave-owners in the South, more than 200,000 owned five slaves or less, and 88 per cent of all the owners held less than twenty slaves each. Describing the plantation system, the historian John Hope Franklin has written:

> The great majority of the plantations were managed by the planters themselves. An overseer would not be needed unless there were more than twenty slaves or unless the planter was an absentee landlord . . . It was on the plantations where there were overseers that the greatest amount of cruelty and brutality existed. Too frequently they hated the system and directed a special contempt toward the Negro, because they were of the opinion that Negro slavery was responsible for their unfortunate economic plight . . . The owners demanded that overseers get work out of the slaves and produce a superior crop. With such a mandate the overseers were ruthless and excessively cruel in their treatment of slaves. Frequently, fights grew out of attempts to punish slaves; and in several instances the overseers were run off the plantations by irate slaves . . . On some plantations a Negro, called the driver, was selected to assist the owner or overseer in getting work out of the slaves. The other workers frequently resented this delegation of authority to one among them, and the driver

was sometimes viewed by the slaves as a traitor, especially if he took his duties seriously.

The autobiography of Josiah Henson, from which the following story is taken, was one of the most widely read slave narratives of the nineteenth century, partly because Henson was identified with the title character in Harriet Beecher Stowe's bestselling novel *Uncle Tom's Cabin*. Like many literary legends, this one is not entirely accurate. Mrs. Stowe had read and drawn upon the entire range of slave narrative literature and interviews with former slaves that were popular at the time. *The Life of Josiah Henson, Formerly a Slave Now an Inhabitant of Canada* was first published in Boston in 1849, and a substantially revised edition, entitled *Truth Stranger than Fiction: Father Henson's Story of His Own Life*, was published in Boston in 1858, and in London in 1859. This second edition, from which the following selection was taken, is believed to have been written by Josiah Henson himself; the first edition of his life was narrated by him to an editor and a later third edition, "revised and enlarged" and republished many times, included elaborate editions and revisions which were not by him.

Father Henson's Story

EARLIEST MEMORIES (FROM CHAPTER 1)

I was born June 15th, 1789, in Charles county, Maryland, on a farm belonging to Mr. Francis Newman, about a mile from Port Tobacco. My mother was a slave of Dr. Josiah McPherson, but hired to the Mr. Newman to whom my father belonged. The only incident I can remember which occurred while my mother continued on Mr. Newman's farm, was the appearance one day of my father with his head bloody and

his back lacerated. He was beside himself with mingled rage
and suffering. The explanation I picked up from the conversation of others only partially explained the matter to my mind;
but as I grew older I understood it all. It seemed the overseer
had sent my mother away from the other field hands to a retired place, and after trying persuasion in vain, had resorted
to force to accomplish a brutal purpose. Her screams aroused
my father at his distant work, and running up, he found his
wife struggling with the man. Furious at the sight, he sprung
upon him like a tiger. In a moment the overseer was down,
and, mastered by rage, my father would have killed him but
for the entreaties of my mother, and the overseer's own promise that nothing should ever be said of the matter. The promise
was kept—like most promises of the cowardly and debased—
as long as the danger lasted.

The laws of slave states provide means and opportunities
for revenge so ample, that miscreants like him never fail to
improve them. "A nigger has struck a white man;" that is
enough to set a whole county on fire; no question is asked
about the provocation. The authorities were soon in pursuit
of my father. The fact of the sacrilegious act of lifting a hand
against the sacred temple of a white man's body—a profanity
as blasphemous in the eye of a slave-state tribunal as was
among the Jews the entrance of a Gentile dog into the Holy
of Holies—this was all it was necessary to establish. And the
penalty followed: one hundred lashes on the bare back, and
to have the right ear nailed to the whipping-post, and then
severed from the body. For a time my father kept out of the
way, hiding in the woods, and at night venturing into some
cabin in search of food. But at length the strict watch set
baffled all his efforts. His supplies cut off, he was fairly
starved out, and compelled by hunger to come back and give
himself up.

The day for the execution of the penalty was appointed. The
negroes from the neighboring plantations were summoned, for

The purchaser of the husband has sent to have him dragged away. As he does not wish for the 'balance' of the family, they have been taken by different purchasers. See page 33.

12 Viewing human beings as property, the American slave laws denied slaves any marital or parental rights and possibilities of constituting families. This aspect of slavery was attacked repeatedly in abolitionist literature, as seen here in the *American Anti-Slavery Almanac for 1838*

their moral improvement, to witness the scene. A powerful blacksmith named Hewes laid on the stripes. Fifty were given, during which the cries of my father might be heard a mile, and then a pause ensued. True, he had struck a white man, but as valuable property he must not be damaged. Judicious men felt his pulse. Oh! he could stand the whole. Again and again the thong fell on his lacerated back. His cries grew fainter and fainter, till a feeble groan was the only response to the final blows. His head was then thrust against the post, and his right ear fastened to it with a tack; a swift pass of a knife, and the bleeding member was left sticking to the place. Then came a hurrah from the degraded crowd, and the exclamation, "That's what he's got for striking a white man." A few said, "it's a damned shame;" but the majority regarded it as a proper tribute to their offended majesty.

It may be difficult for you, reader, to comprehend such brutality; and in the name of humanity you may protest against the truth of these statements. To you, such cruelty inflicted on a man seems fiendish. Ay, on a *man;* there hinges the whole. In the estimation of the illiterate, besotted poor whites who constituted the witnesses of such scenes in Charles County, Maryland, the man who did not feel rage enough at hearing of "a nigger" striking a white to be ready to burn him alive, was only fit to be lynched out of the neighborhood. A blow at one white man is a blow at all. . . .

Previous to this affair my father, from all I can learn, had been a good-humored and light-hearted man, the ringleader in all fun at corn-huskings and Christmas buffoonery. His banjo was the life of the farm, and all night long at a merry-making would he play on it while the other negroes danced. But from this hour he became utterly changed. Sullen, morose, and dogged, nothing could be done with him. . . . So off he was sent to Alabama. What was his after fate neither my mother nor I have ever learned. . . .

ESCAPE FROM BONDAGE (FROM CHAPTER 12)

Canada was often spoken of as the only sure refuge from pursuit, and that blessed land was now the desire of my longing heart. Infinite toils and perils lay between me and that haven of promise; enough to daunt the stoutest heart; but the fire behind me was too hot and fierce to let me pause to consider them. I knew the North Star—blessed be God for setting it in the heavens! . . . I knew that it had led thousands of my poor, hunted brethren to freedom and blessedness. I felt energy enough in my own breast to contend with privation and danger; and had I been a free, untrammeled man, knowing no tie of father or husband, and concerned for my own safety only, I would have felt all difficulties light in view of the hope that was set before me. But, alas! I had a wife and four dear children; how should I provide for them? They, too, must share with me the life of liberty.

It was not without long thought upon the subject that I devised a plan of escape. But at last I matured it. My mind fully made up, I communicated the intention to my wife. She was overwhelmed with terror. . . . With tears and supplications she besought me to remain at home, contented. In vain I explained to her our liability to be torn asunder at any moment; the horrors of the slavery I had lately seen; the happiness we should enjoy together in a land of freedom, safe from all pursuing harm. She had not suffered the bitterness of my lot, nor felt the same longing for deliverance. . . .

I argued the matter with her at various times, till I was satisfied that argument alone would not prevail. I then told her deliberately, that though it would be a cruel trial for me to part with her, I would nevertheless do it, and take all the children with me except the youngest, rather than remain at home, only to be forcibly torn from her, and sent down to linger out a wretched existence in the hell I had lately visited. Again she wept and entreated, but I was sternly resolute. The

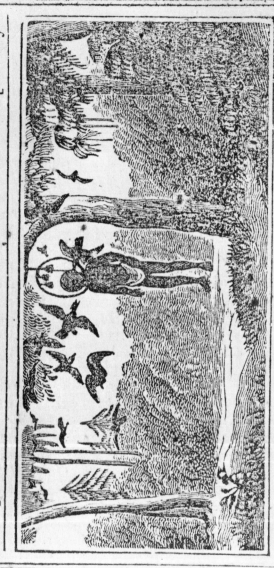

The slave Paul had suffered so much in slavery, that he chose to encounter the hardships and perils of a runaway. He exposed himself, in gloomy forests, to cold and starvation, and finally hung himself, that he might not again fall into the hands of his tormentor. [See Ball's Narrative, 2d Edit. p. 325.]

13 Braving the perils of capture and death, tens of thousands of slaves resisted slavery by running away. The runaway was a heroic symbol of resistance and martyrdom to the abolitionists

whole night long she fruitlessly urged me to relent; exhausted and maddened, I left her, in the morning, to go to my work for the day. Before I had gone far, I heard her voice calling me, and waiting till I came up, she said, at last, she would go with me. Blessed relief! my tears of joy flowed faster than had hers of grief.

Our cabin, at this time, was near the landing. The plantation itself extended the whole five miles from the house to the river. There were several distinct farms, all of which I was over-seeing, and therefore I was riding about from one to another every day. Our oldest boy was at the house with Master Amos; the rest of the children were with my wife.

The chief practical difficulty that had weighed upon my mind, was connected with the youngest two of the children. They were of three and two years, respectively, and of course would have to be carried. Both stout and healthy, they were a heavy burden, and my wife had declared that I should break down under it before I had got five miles from home. Sometime previously I had directed her to make me a large knapsack of tow cloth, large enough to hold them both, and arranged with strong straps to go round my shoulders. This done, I had practised carrying them night after night, both to test my own strength and accustom them to submit to it. To them it was fine fun, and to my great joy I found I could manage them successfully. My wife's consent was given on Thursday morning, and I resolved to start on the night of the following Saturday. Sunday was a holiday; on Monday and Tuesday I was to be away on farms distant from the house; thus several days would elapse before I should be missed, and by that time I should have got a good start. : . .

It was about the middle of September, and by nine o'clock all was ready. It was a dark, moonless night, when we got into the little skiff, in which I had induced a fellow slave to set us across the river. It was an anxious moment. We sat still as death. In the middle of the stream the good fellow said to me, "It will be the end of me if this is ever found out; but you won't be brought back alive, Sie, will you?" "Not if I can help it," I replied; and I thought of the pistols and knife I had bought some time before of a poor white. "And if they're too many for you, and you get seized, you'll never tell my part in this business?" "Not if I'm shot through like a sieve." "That's all," said he, "and God help you." Heaven reward him. He, too, has since followed in my steps; and many a time in a land of freedom have we talked over that dark night on the river. . . .

For a fortnight we pressed steadily on, keeping to the road during the night, hiding whenever a chance vehicle or horseman was heard, and during the day burying ourselves in the woods. Our provisions were rapidly giving out. Two days before reaching Cincinnati they were utterly exhausted. All night long the children cried with hunger, and my poor wife loaded me with reproaches for bringing them into such misery. It was a bitter thing to hear them cry, and God knows I needed encouragement myself. My limbs were weary, and my back and shoulders raw with the burden I carried. A fearful dread of detection ever pursued me, and I would start out of my sleep in terror, my heart beating against my ribs, expecting to find the dogs and slave-hunters after me. Had I been alone I would have borne starvation, even to exhaustion, before I would have ventured in sight of a house in quest of food. But now something must be done; it was necessary to run the risk of exposure by daylight upon the road.

The only way to proceed was to adopt a bold course. Accordingly, I left our hiding-place, took to the road, and turned towards the south, to lull any suspicion that might be aroused were I to be seen going the other way. Before long I came to a house. A furious dog rushed out at me, and his master following to quiet him, I asked if he would sell me a little bread and meat. He was a surly fellow. "No, he had nothing for niggers!" At the next I succeeded no better, at first. The man of the house met me in the same style; but his wife, hearing our conversation, said to her husband, "How can you treat any human being so? If a dog was hungry I would give him something to eat." She then added, "We have children, and who knows but they may some day need the help of a friend." The man laughed, and told her that she might take care of niggers, he wouldn't. She asked me to come in, loaded a plate with venison and bread, and, when I laid it into my handkerchief, and put a quarter of a dollar on the table, she quietly took it up and put it in my handkerchief, with an additional quantity of venison. I felt the hot tears roll down my cheeks as she said "God bless you;" and I hurried away to bless my starving wife and little ones.

A little while after eating the venison, which was quite salt, the children become very thirsty, and groaned and sighed so that I went off stealthily, breaking the bushes to keep my path, to find water. I found a little rill, and drank a large draught. Then I tried to carry some in my hat; but, alas! it leaked. Finally, I took off both shoes, which luckily had no holes in them, rinsed them out, filled them with water, and carried it to my family. They drank it with great delight. I have since then sat at splendidly furnished tables in Canada, the United States, and England; but never did I see any human beings relish anything more than my poor famishing little ones did that refreshing draught out of their father's shoes. That night we made a long run, and two days afterward we reached Cincinnati.

JOURNEY TO CANADA (FROM CHAPTER 13)

I now felt comparatively at home. Before entering the town I hid my wife and children in the woods, and then walked on alone in search of my friends. They welcomed me warmly, and just after dusk my wife and children were brought in, and we found ourselves hospitably cheered and refreshed. Two weeks of exposure to incessant fatigue, anxiety, rain, and chill, made it indescribably sweet to enjoy once more the comfort of rest and shelter. . . .

We followed the same course as before—travelling by night and resting by day—till we arrived at the Scioto, where we had been told we should strike the military road of General Hull, in the last war with Great Britain, and might then safely travel by day. We found the road, accordingly, by the large sycamore and elms which marked its beginning, and entered upon it with fresh spirits early in the day. Nobody had told us that it was cut through the wilderness, and I had neglected to provide any food, thinking we should soon come to some habitation, where we could be supplied. But we travelled on all day without seeing one, and lay down at night, hungry and weary enough. The wolves were howling around us, and though too cowardly to approach, their noise terrified my poor wife and children. Nothing remained to us in the morning but a little piece of dried beef, too little, indeed, to satisfy our cravings, but enough to afflict us with intolerable thirst. I divided most of this among us, and then we started for a second day's tramp in the wilderness. A painful day it was to us. The road was rough, the underbrush tore our clothes and exhausted our strength; trees that had been blown down blocked the way; we were faint with hunger; and no prospect of relief opened up before us. We spoke little, but steadily struggled along; I with my babes on my back, my wife aiding the two other children to climb over the fallen trunks and force themselves through the briers. Suddenly, as I was plodding along a little ahead of my wife and the boys, I heard them call me, and turning round saw my wife prostrate on the ground. "Mother's dying," cried Tom; and when I reached her it seemed really so. From sheer exhaustion she had fallen in surmounting a log. Distracted with anxiety, I feared she was gone. For some minutes no sign of life was manifest; but after a time she opened her eyes, and finally recovering enough

14 Runaway slaves had to evade the vast number of "patrollers" constantly scouring the South. Many never did

to take a few mouthfuls of the beef, her strength returned, and we once more went bravely on our way. I cheered the sad group with hopes I was far from sharing myself. For the first time I was nearly ready to abandon myself to despair. Starvation in the wilderness was the doom that stared me and mine in the face. But again, "man's extremity was God's opportunity."

We had not gone far, and I suppose it was about three o'clock in the afternoon, when we discerned some persons approaching us at no great distance. We were instantly on the alert, as we could hardly expect them to be friends. The advance of a few paces showed me they were Indians, with packs on their shoulders; and they were so near that if they were hostile it would be useless to try to escape. So I walked along boldly, till we came close upon them. They were bent down with their burdens, and had not raised their eyes till now; and when they did so, and saw me coming towards them, they looked at me in a frightened sort of way for a moment, and then, setting up a peculiar howl, turned round, and ran as fast as they could. There were three or four of them, and what they were afraid of I could not imagine, unless they supposed I was the devil, whom they had perhaps heard of as black. But, even then, one would have thought my wife and children might have reässured them. However, there was no doubt they were well frightened, and we heard their wild and prolonged howl, as they ran, for a mile or more. My wife was alarmed, too, and thought they were merely running back to collect more of a party, and then to come and murder us; and she wanted to turn back. I told her they were numerous enough to do that, if they wanted to, without help; and that as for turning back, I had had quite too much of the road behind us, and that it would be a ridiculous thing that both parties should run away. If they were disposed to run, I would follow. We did follow, and the noise soon ceased. As we advanced, we could discover Indians peeping at us from behind the trees, and dodging out of sight if they thought we were looking at them. Presently we came upon their wigwams, and saw a fine-looking, stately Indian, with his arms folded, waiting for us to approach. He was, apparently, the chief; and, saluting us civilly, he soon discovered we were human beings, and spoke to his young men, who were scattered about, and made them come in and give up their foolish fears. And now curiosity seemed to prevail. Each one wanted to touch the children, who were as shy as partridges with their long life in the woods; and as they shrunk away, and uttered a little cry of alarm, the Indian would jump back too, as if he thought they would bite him. However, a little while sufficed to make them understand what we were, and whither we were going, and what we needed; and as little to set them about supplying our wants, feeding us bountifully, and giving us a comfortable wigwam for our night's rest. The next day we resumed our march, having ascertained from the Indians that we were only about twenty-five miles from the lake. They sent some of their young men to point out the place where we were to turn off, and parted from us with as much kindness as possible.

In passing over the part of Ohio near the lake, where such an extensive plain is found, we came to a spot overflowed by a stream, across which the road passed. I forded it first, with the help of a sounding-pole, and then taking the children on my back, first the two little ones, and then the others, one at a time, and, lastly, my wife, I succeeded in getting them safely across. At this time the skin was worn from my back to an extent almost equal to the size of the knapsack.

One night more was passed in the woods, and in the course of the next forenoon we came out upon the wide plain, without trees, which lies south and west of Sandusky city. The houses of the village were in plain sight. About a mile from the lake I hid my wife and children in the bushes, and pushed forward. I was attracted by a house on the left, between which and a small coasting vessel a number of men were passing and repassing with great activity. Promptly deciding to approach them, I drew near, and scarcely had I come within hailing distance, when the captain of the schooner cried out, "Hollo there, man! you want to work?" "Yes, sir!" shouted I. "Come along, come along; I'll give you a shilling an hour. Must get off with this wind." As I came near, he said, "O, you can't work; you're crippled." "Can't I?" said I; and in a minute I had hold of a bag of corn, and followed the gang in emptying it into the hold. I took my place in the line of laborers next to a colored man, and soon got into conversation with him. "How far is it to Canada?" He gave me a peculiar look, and in a minute I saw he knew all. "Want to go to Canada? Come along with us, then. Our captain's a fine fellow. We're going to Buffalo." "Buffalo; how far is that from Canada?" "Don't you know, man? Just across the river." I now opened my mind frankly to him, and told him about my wife and children. "I'll speak to the captain," said he. He did so, and in a moment the captain took me aside, and said, "The Doctor says you want to go to Buffalo with your family." "Yes, sir." "Well, why not go with me!" was his frank reply. "Doctor says you've got a family." "Yes sir." "Where do you stop?" "About a mile back." "How long have you been here?" "No time," I answered, after a moment's hesitation. "Come, my good fellow, tell us all about it. You're running away, ain't you?" I saw he was a friend, and opened my heart to him. "How long will it take you to get ready?" "Be here in half an hour, sir." "Well, go along and get them." Off I started; but, before I had run fifty feet, he called me back. "Stop," says he; "you go on getting the grain in. When we get off, I'll lay to over opposite that island, and send a boat back. There's a lot of regular nigger-catchers in the town below, and they might suspect if you brought your party out of the bush by daylight." I worked away with a will. Soon the two or three hundred bushels of corn were aboard, the hatches fastened down, the anchor raised, and the sails hoisted.

I watched the vessel with intense interest as she left her moorings. Away she went before the free breeze. Already she seemed beyond the spot at which the captain agreed to lay to, and still she flew along. My heart sunk within me; so near deliverance, and again to have my hopes blasted, again to be cast on my own resources. I felt that they had been making a mock of my misery. The sun had sunk to rest, and the purple and gold of the west were fading away into grey. Suddenly, however, as I gazed with weary heart, the vessel swung round into the wind, the sails flapped, and she stood motionless. A moment more, and a boat was lowered from her stern, and with steady stroke made for the point at which I stood. I felt that my hour of release had come. On she came, and in ten minutes she rode up handsomely on to the beach.

My black friend and two sailors jumped out, and we started off at once for my wife and children. To my horror, they were gone from the place where I left them. Overpowered with fear, I supposed they had been found and carried off. There was no time to lose, and the men told me I would have to go alone. Just at the point of despair, however, I stumbled on one of the children. My wife, it seemed, alarmed at my long absence, had given up all for lost, and supposed I had fallen into the hands of the enemy. When she heard my voice, mingled with those of the others she thought my captors were leading me back to make me discover my family, and in the extremity of her terror she had tried to hide herself. I had hard work to satisfy her. Our long habits of concealment and anxiety had rendered her suspicious of every one; and her agitation was so great that for a time she was incapable of understanding what I said, and went on in a sort of paroxysm of distress and fear. This, however, was soon over, and the kindness of my companions did much to facilitate the matter.

And now we were off for the boat. It required little time to embark our baggage—one convenience, at least, of having nothing. The men bent their backs with a will, and headed steadily for a light hung from the vessel's mast. I was praising God in my soul. Three hearty cheers welcomed us as we reached the schooner, and never till my dying day shall I forget the shout of the captain—he was a Scotchman— "Coom up on deck, and clop your wings and craw like a rooster; you're a free nigger as sure as the devil.". . .

ELIZABETH KECKLEY

In addition to all the other hardships of slavery, slave women had to suffer the sexual advances of their owners and other white men who felt they could do as they pleased with them. Many of the narratives written by women who had been slaves exposed this aspect of slave life.

Elizabeth Keckley was a remarkable woman who wrote one of the important narratives published after the Civil War. She was born in Virginia, was a slave in Virginia and North Carolina for thirty years, and succeeded finally in purchasing her freedom from her last master on the basis of her own earnings as a seamstress and modiste. After she was free she went to Washington and secured a position in the White House while Abraham Lincoln was president. She became a close associate and friend of Mrs Lincoln. She wrote an autobiography which is both a story of her life as a slave and a source of historical information on events at the White House during the Lincoln administration. It was published in 1868 in New York and was entitled *Behind the Scenes, or, Thirty Years a Slave, and Four Years in the White House*. The selection that follows is from the earliest chapters of the book, depicting her life as a slave.

The Sorrows of Girlhood

I   WHERE I WAS BORN

My life has been an eventful one. I was born a slave—was the child of slave parents—therefore I came upon the earth free in

God-like thought, but fettered in action. My birthplace was Dinwiddie Court-House, in Virginia. My recollections of childhood are distinct, perhaps for the reason that many stirring incidents are associated with that period. I am now on the shady side of forty, and as I sit alone in my room the brain is busy, and a rapidly moving panorama brings scene after scene before me, some pleasant and others sad; and when I thus greet old familiar faces, I often find myself wondering if I am not living the past over again. As I cannot condense, I must omit many strange passages in my history. From such a wilderness of events it is difficult to make a selection, but as I am not writing altogether the history of myself, I will confine my story to the most important incidents which I believe influenced the moulding of my character. I presume that I must have been four years old when I first began to remember; at least, I cannot now recall anything occurring previous to this period. My master, Col. A. Burwell, was somewhat unsettled in his business affairs, and while I was yet an infant he made several removals. While living at Hampton Sidney College, Prince Edward County, Va., Mrs. Burwell gave birth to a daughter, a sweet, black-eyed baby, my earliest and fondest pet. To take care of this baby was my first duty. True, I was but a child myself—only four years old—but then I had been raised in a hardy school—had been taught to rely upon myself, and to prepare myself to render assistance to others. The lesson was not a bitter one, for I was too young to indulge in philosophy, and the precepts that I then treasured and practised I believe developed those principles of character which have enabled me to triumph over so many difficulties. Notwithstanding all the wrongs that slavery heaped upon me, I can bless it for one thing—youth's important lesson of self-reliance. The baby was named Elizabeth, and it was pleasant to me to be assigned a duty in connection with it, for the discharge of that duty transferred me from the rude cabin to the household of my master. My simple attire was a short dress and a little white apron. My old mistress encouraged me in rocking the cradle, by telling me that if I would watch over the baby well, keep the flies out of its face, and not let it cry, I should be its little maid. This was a golden promise, and I required no better inducement for the faithful performance of my task. I began to rock the cradle most industriously, when lo! out pitched little pet on the floor. I instantly cried out, "Oh! the baby is on the floor;" and, not knowing what to do, I seized the fire-shovel in my perplexity, and was trying to shovel up my tender charge, when my mistress called to me to let the child alone, and then ordered that I be taken out and lashed for my carelessness. The blows were not administered with a light hand, I assure you, and doubtless the severity of the lashing has made me remember the incident so well. This was the first time I was punished in this cruel way, but not the last. The black-eyed baby that I called my pet grew into a self-willed girl, and in after years was the cause of much trouble to me. I grew strong and healthy, and, notwithstanding I knit socks and attended to various kinds of work, I was repeatedly told, when even fourteen years old, that I would never be worth my salt. When I was eight, Mr. Burwell's family consisted of six sons and four daughters, with a large family of servants. My mother was kind and forbearing; Mrs. Burwell a hard task-master; and as mother had so much work to do in making clothes, etc., for the family, besides the slaves, I determined to render her all the assistance in my power, and in rendering her such assistance my young energies were taxed to the utmost. I was my mother's only child, which made her love for me all the stronger. I did not know much of my father, for he was the slave of another man, and when Mr. Burwell moved from Dinwiddie he was separated from us, and only allowed to visit my mother twice a year—during the Easter holidays and Christmas. At last Mr. Burwell determined to reward my mother, by making an arrangement with the owner of my father, by which the separation of my parents could be brought to an end. It was a bright day, indeed, for my mother when it was announced that my father was coming to live with us. The old weary look faded from her face, and she worked as if her heart was in every task. But the golden days did not last long. The radiant dream faded all too soon.

In the morning my father called me to him and kissed me, then held me out at arms' length as if he were regarding his child with pride. "She is growing into a large fine girl," he remarked to my mother. "I dun no which I like best, you or Lizzie, as both are so dear to me." My mother's name was Agnes, and my father delighted to call me his "Little Lizzie." While yet my father and mother were speaking hopefully, joyfully of the future, Mr. Burwell came to the cabin, with a letter in his hand. He was a kind master in some things, and as gently as possible informed my parents that they must part; for in two hours my father must join his master at Dinwiddie and go with him to the West, where he had determined to make his future home. The announcement fell upon the little circle in that rude-log cabin like a thunderbolt. I can remember the scene as if it were but yesterday;—how my father cried out against the cruel separation; his last kiss; his wild straining of my mother to his bosom; the solemn prayer to Heaven; the tears and sobs—the fearful anguish of broken hearts. The last kiss, last good-by; and he, my father, was gone, gone forever. The shadow eclipsed the sunshine, and love brought despair. The parting was eternal. The cloud had no silver lining, but I trust that it will be all silver in heaven. We who are crushed to earth with heavy chains, who travel a weary, rugged, thorny road, groping through midnight darkness on earth, earn our right to enjoy the sunshine in the great hereafter. At the grave, at least, we should be permitted to lay our burdens down, that a new world, a world of brightness, may open to us. The light that is denied us here should grow into a flood of effulgence beyond the dark, mysterious shadows of death. Deep as was the distress of my mother in parting with my father, her sorrow did not screen her from insult. My old mistress said to her: "Stop your nonsense; there is no necessity for you putting on airs. Your husband is not the only slave that has been sold from his family, and you are not the only one that has had to part. There are plenty more men about here, and if you want a husband so badly, stop your crying and go and find another." To these unfeeling words my mother made no reply. She turned away in stoical silence, with a curl of that loathing scorn upon her lips which swelled in her heart.

My father and mother never met again in this world. They kept up a regular correspondence for years, and the most precious mementoes of my existence are the faded old letters that he wrote, full of love, and always hoping that the future would bring brighter days. In nearly every letter is a message for me. "Tell my darling little Lizzie," he writes, "to be a good girl, and to learn her book. Kiss her for me, and tell her that I will come to see her some day." Thus he wrote time and again, but he never came. He lived in hope, but died without ever seeing his wife and child.

I note a few extracts from one of my father's letters to my mother, following copy literally:

"SHELBYVILE, Sept. 6, 1833.
"MRS. AGNES HOBBS.

"Dear Wife: My dear biloved wife I am more than glad to meet with opportunty writee thes few lines to you by my Mistress who ar now about starterng to virginia, and sevl others of my old friends are with her; in compeney Mrs. Ann Rus the wife of master Thos Rus and Dan Woodiard and his family and I am very sorry that I havn the chance to go with them as I feele Determid to see you If life last again. I am now here and out at this pleace so I am not abble to get of at this time. I am write well and hearty and all the rest of masters family. I heard this eveng by Mistress that ar just from theree all sends love to you and all my old frends. I am a living in a town called Shelbyville and I have wrote a greate many letters since Ive beene here and almost been reeady to my selfe that its out of the question to write any more at tall: my dear wife I dont feeld no whys like

How do you like this — You d——d Negro Stealer

LOOK OUT.

The undersigned would announce to the public generally, that he has a splendid lot of well broke

NEGRO DOGS,

And will attend at any reasonable distance, to the catching of runaways, at the lowest possible rates. All those having slaves in the woods will do well to address

W. D. GILBERT,

Jan. 29, 1856.   Franklin, Simpson co. Ky.

[N. B. Please post this up in a conspicuous place.]

15 Slave-catching and the special training of hounds to track down runaways were a regular business in the South. This advertising handbill was tauntingly sent to the Reverend Theodore Parker, the famous Unitarian abolitionist, with some handwritten namecalling

giving out writing to you as yet and I hope when you get this letter that you be Inncougege to write me a letter. I am well satisfied at my living at this place I am a making money for my own benifit and I hope that its to yours also If I live to see Nexct year I shall heve my own time from master by giving him 100 and twenty Dollars a year and I thinke I shall be doing good bisness at that and heve something more thean all that. I hope with gods helpe that I may be abble to rejoys with you on the earth and In heaven lets meet when will I am detemnid to nuver stope praying, not in this earth and I hope to praise god In glory there weel meet to part no more forever. So my dear wife I hope to meet you In paradase to prase god forever * * * * * I want Elizabeth to be a good girl and not to thinke that becasue I am bound so fare that gods not abble to open the way * * * *

"GEORGE PLEASANT,
"*Hobbs a servant of Grum.*"

The last letter that my mother received from my father was dated Shelbyville, Tennessee, March 20, 1839. He writes in a cheerful strain, and hopes to see her soon. Alas! he looked forward to a meeting in vain. Year after year the one great hope swelled in his heart, but the hope was only realized beyond the dark portals of the grave.

When I was about seven years old I witnessed, for the first time, the sale of a human being. We were living at Prince Edward, in Virginia, and master had just purchased his hogs for the winter, for which he was unable to pay in full. To escape from his embarrassment it was necessary to sell one of the slaves. Little Joe, the son of the cook, was selected as the victim. His mother was ordered to dress him up in his Sunday clothes, and send him to the house. He came in with a bright face, was placed in the scales, and was sold, like the hogs, at so much per pound. His mother was kept in ignorance of the transaction, but her suspicions were aroused. When her son started for Petersburgh in the wagon, the truth began to dawn upon her mind, and she pleaded piteously that her boy should not be taken from her; but master quieted her by telling her that he was simply going to town with the wagon, and would be back in the morning. Morning came, but little Joe did not return to his mother. Morning after morning passed, and the mother went down to the grave without ever seeing her child again. One day she was whipped for grieving for her lost boy. Colonel Burwell never liked to see one of his slaves wear a sorrowful face, and those who offended in this particular way were always punished. Alas! the sunny face of the slave is not always an indication of sunshine in the heart. Colonel Burwell at one time owned about seventy slaves, all of which were sold, and in a majority of instances wives were separated from husbands and children from their parents. Slavery in the Border States forty years ago was different from what it was twenty years ago. Time seemed to soften the hearts of master and mistress, and to insure kinder and more humane treatment to bondsmen and bondswomen. When I was quite a child, an incident occurred which my mother afterward impressed more strongly on my mind. One of my uncles, a slave of Colonel Burwell, lost a pair of ploughlines, and when the loss was made known the master gave him a new pair, and told him that if he did not take care of them he would punish him severely. In a few weeks the second pair of lines was stolen, and my uncle hung himself rather than meet the displeasure of his master. My mother went to the spring in the morning for a pail of water, and on looking up into the willow tree which shaded the bubbling crystal stream, she discovered the lifeless form of her brother suspended beneath one of the strong branches. Rather than be punished the way Colonel Burwell punished his servants, he took his own life. Slavery had its dark side as well as its bright side.

II GIRLHOOD AND ITS SORROWS

I must pass rapidly over the stirring events of my early life. When I was about fourteen years old I went to live with my master's eldest son, a Presbyterian minister. His salary was small, and he was burdened with a helpless wife, a girl that he had married in the humble walks of life. She was morbidly sensitive, and imagined that I regarded her with contemptuous feelings because she was of poor parentage. I was their only servant, and a gracious loan at that. They were not able to buy me, so my old master sought to render them assistance by allowing them the benefit of my services. From the very first I did the work of three servants, and yet I was scolded and regarded with distrust. The years passed slowly, and I continued to serve them, and at the same time grew into strong, healthy womanhood. I was nearly eighteen when we removed from Virginia to Hillsboro', North Carolina, where young Mr. Burwell took charge of a church. The salary was small, and we still had to practise the closest economy. Mr. Bingham, a hard, cruel man, the village schoolmaster, was a member of my young master's church, and he was a frequent visitor to the parsonage. She whom I called mistress seemed to be desirious to wreak vengeance on me for something, and Bingham became her ready tool. During this time my master was unusually kind to me; he was naturally a good-hearted man, but was influenced by his wife. It was Saturday evening, and while I was bending over the bed, watching the baby that I had just hushed into slumber, Mr. Bingham came to the door and asked me to go with him to his study. Wondering what he meant by his strange request, I followed him, and when we had entered the study he closed the door, and in his blunt way remarked: "Lizzie, I am going to flog you." I was thunderstruck, and tried to think if I had been remiss in anything. I could not recollect of doing anything to deserve punishment, and with surprise exclaimed: "Whip me, Mr. Bingham! what for?"

"No matter," he replied, "I am going to whip you, so take down your dress this instant."

Recollect, I was eighteen years of age, was a woman fully developed, and yet this man coolly bade me take down my dress. I drew myself up proudly, firmly, and said: "No, Mr. Bingham, I shall not take down my dress before you. Moreover, you shall not whip me unless you prove the stronger. Nobody has a right to whip me but my own master, and nobody shall do so if I can prevent it."

My words seemed to exasperate him. He seized a rope, caught me roughly, and tried to tie me. I resisted with all my strength, but he was the stronger of the two, and after a hard struggle succeeded in binding my hands and tearing my dress from my back. Then he picked up a rawhide, and began to ply it freely over my shoulders. With steady hand and practised eye he would raise the instrument of torture, nerve himself for a blow, and with fearful force the rawhide descended upon the quivering flesh. It cut the skin, raised great welts, and the warm blood trickled down my back. Oh God! I can feel the torture now—the terrible, excruciating agony of those moments. I did not scream; I was too proud to let my tormentor know what I was suffering. I closed my lips firmly, that not even a groan might escape from them, and I stood like a statue while the keen lash cut deep into my flesh. As soon as I was released, stunned with pain, bruised and bleeding, I went home and rushed into the presence of the pastor and his wife, wildly exclaiming: "Master Robert, why did you let Mr. Bingham flog me? What have I done that I should be so punished?"

"Go away," he gruffly answered, "do not bother me."

I would not be put off thus. "What *have* I done? I *will* know why I have been flogged."

I saw his cheeks flush with anger, but I did not move. He rose to his feet, and on my refusing to go without an explanation, seized a chair, struck me, and felled me to the floor. I rose, bewildered, almost dead with pain, crept to my room, dressed my bruised arms and back as best I could, and then lay down, but not to sleep. No, I could not sleep, for I was suffering mental as well as bodily torture. My spirit rebelled against the unjustness that had been inflicted upon me, and though I tried to smother my anger and to forgive those who had been so cruel to me, it was impossible. The next morning I was more calm, and I believe that I could then have forgiven everything for the sake of one kind word. But the kind word was not proffered, and it may be possible that I grew somewhat wayward and sullen. Though I had faults, I know now, as I felt then, harshness was the poorest inducement for the correction of them. It seems that Mr. Bingham had pledged himself to Mrs. Burwell to subdue what he called my "stubborn pride." On Friday following the Saturday on which I was so savagely beaten, Mr. Bingham again directed me to come to his study. I went, but with the determination to offer resistance should he attempt to flog me again. On entering the room I found him prepared with a new rope and a new cowhide. I told him that I was ready to die, but that he could not conquer me. In struggling with him I bit his finger severely, when he seized a heavy stick and beat me with it in a shameful manner. Again I went home sore and bleeding, but with pride as strong and defiant as ever. The following Thursday Mr. Bingham again tried to conquer me, but in vain. We struggled, and he struck me many savage blows. As I stood bleeding before him, nearly exhausted with his efforts, he burst into tears, and declared that it would be a sin to beat me any more. My suffering at last subdued his hard heart; he asked my forgiveness, and afterwards was an altered man. He was never known to strike one of his servants from that day forward. Mr. Burwell, he who preached the love of Heaven, who glorified the precepts and examples of Christ, who expounded the Holy Scriptures Sabbath after Sabbath from the pulpit, when Mr. Bingham refused to whip me any more, was urged by his wife to punish me himself. One morning he went to the wood-pile, took an oak broom, cut the handle off, and with this heavy handle attempted to conquer me. I fought him, but he proved the strongest. At the sight of my bleeding form, his wife fell upon her knees and begged him to desist. My distress even touched her cold, jealous heart. I was so badly bruised that I was unable to leave my bed for five days. I will not dwell upon the bitter anguish of these hours, for even the thought of them now makes me shudder. The Rev. Mr. Burwell was not yet satisfied. He resolved to make another attempt to subdue my proud, rebellious spirit—made the attempt and again failed, when he told me, with an air of penitence, that he should never strike me another blow; and faithfully he kept his word. These revolting scenes created a great sensation at the time, were the talk of the town and neighbourhood, and I flatter myself that the actions of those who had conspired against me were not viewed in a light to reflect much credit upon them.

The savage efforts to subdue my pride were not the only things that brought me suffering and deep mortification during my residence at Hillsboro'. I was regarded as fair-looking for one of my race, and for four years a white man—I spare the world his name—had base designs upon me. I do not care to dwell upon this subject, for it is one that is fraught with pain. Suffice it to say, that he persecuted me for four years, and I—I— became a mother. The child of which he was the father was the only child that I ever brought into the world. If my poor boy ever suffered any humiliating pangs on account of birth, he could not blame his mother, for God knows that she did not wish to give him life; he must blame the edicts of that society which deemed it no crime to undermine the virtue of girls in my then position. . .

THE REVEREND
HENRY HIGHLAND GARNET

Anti-slavery sentiments are as old as slavery itself. The first printed protest against slavery in America was published by a group of Quakers in Philadelphia in 1693. The Quakers also organized the first anti-slavery society in 1775. By 1792, there were anti-slavery societies in every state from Massachusetts to Virginia. The abolitionist movement, as the militant phase of the anti-slavery movement came to be known, emerged around 1830 and the following years. Descriptions of it have frequently concentrated on White abolitionists, but Black abolitionists were expressing abolitionist ideas and participating in abolitionist actions before the War for Independence of 1776. Among the prominent Black abolitionist writers and spokesmen were David Walker, Frederick Douglass, William Still, William Wells Brown, Reverend Henry Highland Garnet, and many others. More than a score of the Black abolitionists went to England, Scotland, France, and Germany to further the cause of anti-slavery, and among them were three authors included in this book: Reverend Henry Highland Garnet, Frederick Douglass, and William Wells Brown. The abolitionist movement played an important part in the struggle to bring about the termination of slavery.

Henry Highland Garnet was born a slave in 1815, in Maryland. At the age of nine he escaped with his father and mother and a few companions. His family reached Pennsylvania and then moved to New York City and the young Henry attended the New York African Free School, No. 1. He subsequently became a prominent preacher and anti-slavery spokesman and leader. In 1843, at a national convention of Black citizens held in Buffalo, New York, Garnet offered the following "address to the slaves of the United States." It was too radical for the majority of the delegates at that time and was not adopted by the convention, but it remains a landmark of Black anti-slavery literature.

A Former Slave Appeals to the Slaves of the United States of America

BRETHREN AND FELLOW-CITIZENS:—Your brethren of the North, East, and West have been accustomed to meet together in National Conventions, to sympathize with each other, and to weep over your unhappy condition. In these meetings we have addressed all classes of the free, but we have never, until this time, sent a word of consolation and advice to you. We have been contented in sitting still and mourning over your sorrows, earnestly hoping that before this day your sacred liberties would have been restored. But, we have hoped in vain. Years have rolled on, and tens of thousands have been borne on streams of blood and tears, to the shores of eternity. While you have been oppressed, we have also been partakers with you; nor can we be free while you are enslaved. We, therefore, write to you as being bound with you.

Many of you are bound to us, not only by the ties of a common humanity, but we are connected by the more tender relations of parents, wives, husbands, children, brothers, and sisters, and friends. As such we most affectionately address you.

Slavery has fixed a deep gulf between you and us, and while it shuts out from you the relief and consolation which your friends would willingly render, it afflicts and persecutes you with a fierceness which we might not expect to see in the fiends of hell. But still the Almighty Father of mercies has left to us a glimmering ray of hope, which shines out like a lone star in a cloudy sky. Mankind are becoming wiser, and

[1838.] OCTOBER—TENTH MONTH. [31 days.]

THE WAY THEY "CATCH MEN" IN PENNSYLVANIA.

These men having FELT the horrors of slavery, fled to Cambria county, Pa., in April, 1837. Being pursued, one of them said he would die before he would be taken. They were shot and wounded, and then were taken with great difficulty.

16 Reaching the North was no guarantee of freedom for the runaway slaves. Agents of the slave-owners were a menace there, too, as this dramatization shows

better—the oppressor's power is fading, and you, every day, are becoming better informed, and more numerous. Your grievances, brethren, are many. We shall not attempt, in this short address, to present to the world all the dark catalogue of this nation's sins, which have been committed upon an innocent people. Nor is it indeed necessary, for you feel them from day to day, and all the civilized world look upon them with amazement.

Two hundred and twenty-seven years ago, the first of our injured race were brought to the shores of America. They came not with glad spirits to select their homes in the New World. They came not with their own consent, to find an unmolested enjoyment of the blessings of this fruitful soil. The first dealings they had with men calling themselves Christians, exhibited to them the worst features of corrupt and sordid hearts: and convinced them that no cruelty is too great, no villainy and no robbery too abhorrent for even enlightened men to perform, when influenced by avarice and lust. Neither did they come flying upon the wings of Liberty, to a land of freedom. But they came with broken hearts, from their beloved native land, and were doomed to unrequited toil and deep degradation. Nor did the evil of their bondage end at their emancipation by death. Succeeding generations inherited their chains, and millions have come from eternity into time, and have returned again to the world of spirits, cursed and ruined by American slavery.

The propagators of the system, or their immediate ancestors, very soon discovered its growing evil, and its tremendous wickedness, and secret promises were made to destroy it. The gross inconsistency of a people holding slaves, who had themselves "ferried o'er the wave" for freedom's sake, was too apparent to be entirely overlooked. The voice of Freedom cried, "Emancipate your slaves." Humanity supplicated with tears for the deliverance of the children of Africa. Wisdom urged her solemn plea. The bleeding captive plead his innocence, and pointed to Christianity who stood weeping at the cross. Jehovah frowned upon the nefarious institution, and thunderbolts, red with vengeance, struggled to leap forth to blast the guilty wretches who maintained it. But all was vain. Slavery had stretched its dark wings of death over the land, the Church stood silently by—the priests prophesied falsely, and the people loved to have it so. Its throne is established, and now it reigns triumphant.

Nearly three millions of your fellow-citizens are prohibited by law and public opinion, (which in this country is stronger than law,) from reading the Book of Life. Your intellect has been destroyed as much as possible, and every ray of light they have attempted to shut out from your minds. The oppressors themselves have become involved in the ruin. They have become weak, sensual, and rapacious—they have cursed you —they have cursed themselves—they have cursed the earth which they have trod.

The colonist threw the blame upon England. They said that the mother country entailed the evil upon them, and that they would rid themselves of it if they could. The world thought they were sincere, and the philanthropic pitied them. But time soon tested their sincerity. In a few years the colonists grew strong, and severed themselves from the British Government. Their independence was declared, and they took their station among the sovereign powers of the earth. The declaration was a glorious document. Sages admired it, and the patriotic of every nation reverenced the God-like sentiments which it contained. When the power of Government returned to their hands, did they emancipate the slaves? No; they rather added new links to our chains. Were they ignorant of the principles of Liberty? Certainly they were not. The sentiments of their revolutionary orators fell in burning eloquence upon their hearts, and with one voice they cried, LIBERTY OR DEATH. Oh what a sentence was that! It ran from soul to soul like electric fire, and nerved the arm of

thousands to fight in the holy cause of Freedom. Among the
diversity of opinions that are entertained in regard to physical
resistance, there are but a few found to gainsay that stern
declaration. We are among those who do not.

SLAVERY! How much misery is comprehended in that
single word. What mind is there that does not shrink from its
direful effects? Unless the image of God be obliterated from
the soul, all men cherish the love of Liberty. The nice discern-
ing political economist does not regard the sacred right more
than the untutored African who roams in the wilds of Congo.
Nor has the one more right to the full enjoyment of his freedom than the other. In every man's mind the good seeds of
liberty are planted, and he who brings his fellow down so
low, as to make him contented with a condition of slavery,
commits the highest crime against God and man. Brethren,
your oppressors aim to do this. They endeavor to make you
as much like brutes as possible. When they have blinded the
eyes of your mind—when they have embittered the sweet
waters of life—when they have shut out the light which
shines from the word of God—then, and not till then, has
American slavery done its perfect work.

TO SUCH DEGRADATION IT IS SINFUL IN THE EXTREME
FOR YOU TO MAKE VOLUNTARY SUBMISSION. The divine com-
mandments you are in duty bound to reverence and obey. If
you do not obey them, you will surely meet the displeasure of
the Almighty. He requires you to love him supremely, and
your neighbor as yourself—to keep the Sabbath day holy—
to search the Scriptures—and bring up your children with
respect for his laws, and to worship no other God but him.
But slavery sets all these at nought, and hurls defiance in the
face of Jehovah. The forlorn condition in which you are
placed, does not destroy your moral obligation to God. You
are not certain of heaven, because you suffer yourselves to
remain in a state of slavery, where you cannot obey the com-
mandments of the Sovereign of the universe. If the ignorance

of slavery is a passport to heaven, then it is a blessing, and no curse, and you should rather desire its perpetuity than its abolition. God will not receive slavery, nor ignorance, nor any other state of mind, for love and obedience to him. Your condition does not absolve you from your moral obligation. The diabolical injustice by which your liberties are cloven down, NEITHER GOD, NOR ANGELS, OR JUST MEN, COMMAND YOU TO SUFFER FOR A SINGLE MOMENT. THEREFORE IT IS YOUR SOLEMN AND IMPERATIVE DUTY TO USE EVERY MEANS, BOTH MORAL, INTELLECTUAL, AND PHYSICAL, THAT PROM-ISES SUCCESS. If a band of heathen men should attempt to enslave a race of Christians, and to place their children under the influence of some false religion, surely, Heaven would frown upon the men who would not resist such aggression, even to death. If, on the other hand, a band of Christians should attempt to enslave a race of heathen men, and to entail slavery upon them, and to keep them in heathenism in the midst of Christianity, the God of heaven would smile upon every effort which the injured might make to disenthral them-selves.

Brethren, it is as wrong for your lordly oppressors to keep you in slavery, as it was for the man thief to steal our ances-tors, from the coast of Africa. You should therefore now use the same manner of resistance, as would have been just in our ancestors, when the bloody foot-prints of the first remorse-less soul-thief was placed upon the shores of our fatherland. The humblest peasant is as free in the sight of God as the proudest monarch that ever swayed a sceptre. Liberty is a spirit sent out from God, and like its great Author, is no respecter of persons.

Brethren, the time has come when you must act for your-selves. It is an old and true saying that, "if hereditary bond-men would be free, they must themselves strike the blow." You can plead your own cause, and do the work of emancipa-tion better than any others. The nations of the old world are moving in the great cause of universal freedom, and some of them at least will, ere long, do you justice. The combined powers of Europe have placed their broad seal of disapprobation upon the African slave-trade. But in the slave-holding parts of the United States, the trade is as brisk as ever. They buy and sell you as though you were brute beasts. The North has done much—her opinion of slavery in the abstract is known. But in regard to the South, we adopt the opinion of the *New York Evangelist*—"We have advanced so far, that the cause apparently waits for a more effectual door to be thrown open than has been yet." We are about to point you to that more effectual door. Look around you, and behold the bosoms of your loving wives heaving with untold agonies! Hear the cries of your poor children! Remember the stripes your fathers bore. Think of the torture and disgrace of your noble mothers. Think of your wretched sisters, loving virtue and purity, as they are driven into concubinage and are exposed to the unbridled lusts of incarnate devils. Think of the undying glory that hangs around the ancient name of Africa —and forget not that you are native-born American citizens, and as such, you are justly entitled to all the rights that are granted to the freest. Think how many tears you have poured out upon the soil which you have cultivated with unrequited toil and enriched with your blood; and then go to your lordly enslavers and tell them plainly, that you *are determined to be free.* Appeal to their sense of justice, and tell them that they have no more right to oppress you, than you have to enslave them. Entreat them to remove the grievous burdens which they have imposed upon you, and to remunerate you for your labor. Promise them renewed diligence in the cultivation of the soil, if they will render to you an equivalent for your services. Point them to the increase of happiness and prosperity in the British West-Indies since the Act of Emancipation. Tell them in language which they cannot misunderstand, of the exceeding sinfulness of slavery, and of a future judgment, and of the righteous retributions of an indignant God. Inform them that all you desire is FREEDOM, and that nothing else will suffice. Do this, and forever after cease to toil for the heartless tyrants, who give you no other reward but stripes and abuse. If they then commence the work of death, they, and not you, will be responsible for the consequences. You had far better all die—*die immediately,* than live slaves, and entail your wretchedness upon your posterity. If you would be free in this generation, here is your only hope. However much you and all of us may desire it, there is not much hope of redemption without the shedding of blood. If you must bleed, let it all come at once—rather *die freemen, than live to be the slaves.* It is impossible, like the children of Israel, to make a grand exodus from the land of bondage. The Pharoahs are on both sides of the blood-red waters! You cannot move *en masse,* to the dominions of the British Queen—nor can you pass through Florida and overrun Texas, and at last find peace in Mexico. The propagators of American slavery are spending their blood and treasure, that they may plant the black flag in the heart of Mexico and riot in the halls of the Montezumas. In the language of the Rev. Robert Hall, when addressing the volunteers of Bristol, who were rushing forth to repel the invasion of Napoleon, who threatened to lay waste the fair homes of England, "Religion is too much interested in your behalf, not to shed over you her most gracious influences."

You will not be compelled to spend much time in order to become inured to hardships. From the first moment that you breathed the air of heaven, you have been accustomed to nothing else but hardships. The heroes of the American Revolution were never put upon harder fare than a peck of corn and a few herrings per week. You have not become enervated by the luxuries of life. Your sternest energies have been beaten out upon the anvil of severe trial. Slavery has done this, to make you subservient to its own purposes; but it has done more than this, it has prepared you for any emergency. If you receive good treatment, it is what you could hardly expect; if you meet with pain, sorrow, and even death, these are the common lot of the slaves.

Fellow-men! patient sufferers! behold your dearest rights crushed to the earth! See your sons murdered, and your wives, mothers and sisters doomed to prostitution. In the name of the merciful God, and by all that life is worth, let it no longer be a debatable question, whether it is better to choose *Liberty* or *death*.

In 1822, Denmark Veazie, of South Carolina, formed a plan for the liberation of his fellow-men. In the whole history of human efforts to overthrow slavery, a more complicated and tremendous plan was never formed. He was betrayed by the treachery of his own people, and died a martyr to freedom. Many a brave hero fell, but history, faithful to her high trust, will transcribe his name on the same monument with Moses, Hampden, Tell, Bruce and Wallace, Toussaint L'Ouverture, Lafayette and Washington. That tremendous movement shook the whole empire of slavery. The guilty soul-thieves were overwhelmed with fear. It is a matter of fact, that at that time, and in consequence of the threatened revolution, the slave States talked strongly of emancipation. But they blew but one blast of the trumpet of freedom, and then laid it aside. As these men became quiet, the slaveholders ceased to talk about emancipation: and now behold your condition to-day! Angels sigh over it, and humanity has long since exhausted her tears in weeping on your account!

The patriotic Nathaniel Turner followed Denmark Veazie. He was goaded to desperation by wrong and injustice. By despotism, his name has been recorded on the list of infamy, and future generations will remember him among the noble and brave.

Next arose the immortal Joseph Cinque, the hero of the Amistad. He was a native African, and by the help of God he emancipated a whole ship-load of his fellow men on the high seas. And he now sings of liberty on the sunny hills of Africa and beneath his native palm-trees, where he hears the lion roar and feels himself as free as that king of the forest.

Next arose Madison Washington, that bright star of freedom, and took his station in the constellation of true heroism. He was a slave on board the brig Creole, of Richmond, bound to New Orleans, that great slave mart, with a hundred and four others. Nineteen struck for liberty or death. But one life was taken, and the whole were emancipated, and the vessel was carried into Nassau, New Providence.

Noble men! Strike for your lives and liberties. Now is the day and the hour. Let every slave throughout the land do this, and the days of slavery are numbered. You cannot be more oppressed than you have been—you cannot suffer greater cruelties than you have already. *Rather die freemen than live to be slaves.* Remember that you are FOUR MILLIONS!

It is in your power so to torment the God-cursed slaveholders, that they will be glad to let you go free. If the scale was turned, and black men were the masters and white men the slaves, every destructive agent and element would be employed to lay the oppressor low. Danger and death would hang over their heads day and night. Yes, the tyrants would meet with plagues more terrible than those of Pharaoh. But you are a patient people. You act as though you were made for the special use of these devils. You act as though your daughters were born to pamper the lusts of your masters and overseers. And worse than all, you tamely submit while your lords tear your wives from your embraces and defile them before your eyes. In the name of God, we ask, are you men? Where is the blood of your fathers? Has it all run out of your veins? Awake, awake; millions of voices are calling you! Your dead fathers speak to you from their graves. Heaven, as with a voice of thunder, calls on you to arise from the dust.

Let your motto be resistance! *resistance!* RESISTANCE! No oppressed people have ever secured their liberty without resistance. What kind of resistance you had better make, you must decide by the circumstances that surround you, and according to the suggestion of expediency. Brethren, adieu! Trust in the living God. Labor for the peace of the human race, and remember that you are FOUR MILLIONS.

JOURDON ANDERSON

This ironic, tongue-in-cheek letter by a former slave to his former master was originally published in *The Freedmen's Book*, edited by the well-known abolitionist writer Lydia Maria Child and published in Boston in 1865.

Letter from a Freedman to His Old Master
(Written just as he dictated it.)

Dayton, Ohio, August 7, 1865.

To my old Master, Colonel P. H. Anderson, *Big Spring, Tennessee.*

SIR: I got your letter, and was glad to find that you had not forgotten Jourdon, and that you wanted me to come back and live with you again, promising to do better for me than anybody else can. I have often felt uneasy about you. I thought the Yankees would have hung you long before this, for harboring Rebs they found at your house. I suppose they never heard about your going to Colonel Martin's to kill the Union soldier that was left by his company in their stable. Although you shot at me twice before I left you, I did not want to hear of your being hurt, and am glad you are still living. It would do me good to go back to the dear old home again, and see Miss Mary and Miss Martha and Allen, Esther, Green, and Lee. Give my love to them all, and tell them I hope we will meet in the better world, if not in this. I would have gone back to see you all when I was working in the Nashville Hospital, but one of the neighbours told me that Henry intended to shoot me if he ever got a chance.

I want to know particularly what the good chance is you propose to give me. I am doing tolerably well here. I get twenty-five dollars a month, with victuals and clothing; have a comfortable home for Mandy,—the folks call her Mrs. Anderson,—and the children—Milly, Jane, and Grundy— go to school and are learning well. The teacher says Grundy has a head for a preacher. They go to Sunday school, and Mandy and me attend church regularly. We are kindly treated. Sometimes we overhear others saying, "Them colored people were slaves" down in Tennessee. The children feel hurt when they hear such remarks; but I tell them it was no disgrace in Tennessee to belong to Colonel Anderson. Many darkeys would have been proud, as I used to be, to call you master. Now if you will write and say what wages you will give me, I will be better able to decide whether it would be to my advantage to move back again.

As to my freedom, which you say I can have, there is nothing to be gained on that score, as I got my free papers in 1864 from the Provost-Marshal-General of the Department of Nashville. Mandy says she would be afraid to go back without some proof that you were disposed to treat us justly and kindly; and we have concluded to test your sincerity by asking you to send us our wages for the time we served you. This will make us forget and forgive old scores, and rely on your justice and friendship in the future. I served you faithfully for thirty-two years, and Mandy twenty years. At twenty-five dollars a month for me, and two dollars a week for Mandy, our earnings would amount to eleven thousand six hundred and eighty dollars. Add to this the interest for the time our wages have been kept back, and deduct what you paid for our clothing, and three doctor's visits to me, and pulling a tooth for Mandy, and the balance will show what we are in justice entitled to. Please send the money by Adam's Express, in care of V. Winters, Esq., Dayton, Ohio. If you fail to pay us for faithful labors in the past, we can have little faith in your promises in

17 A typical poster offering a reward for the capture of a runaway slave. Numerous reward offers appeared in every issue of newspapers in the South

the future. We trust the good Maker has opened your eyes to the wrongs which you and your fathers have done to me and my fathers, in making us toil for you for generations without recompense. Here I draw my wages every Saturday night; but in Tennessee there was never any pay-day for the negroes any more than for the horses and cows. Surely there will be a day of reckoning for those who defraud the laborer of his hire.

In answering this letter, please state if there would be any safety for my Milly and Jane, who are now grown up, and both good-looking girls. You know how it was with poor Matilda and Catherine. I would rather stay here and starve— and die, if it come to that—than have my girls brought to shame by the violence and wickedness of their young masters. You will also please state if there has been any schools opened for the colored children in your neighborhood. The great desire of my life now is to give my children an education, and have them form virtuous habits.

Say howdy to George Carter, and thank him for taking the pistol from you when you were shooting at me.

From your old servant,
JOURDON ANDERSON.

FREDERICK DOUGLASS

After his escape from slavery in 1838, Frederick Douglass became the most celebrated author of slave narratives, Black
abolitionist leader, Afro-American editor, lecturer, and public
figure. He was a pioneer in developing Afro-American publications to express the point of view and sentiments of the former
slaves and of Black people in America. During his lifetime he
published three different autobiographical books, all classics of
their kind. He was self-taught, read widely, and was a master of
the rhetoric of his time. His autobiographies are readily available in a variety of editions. For this volume I have chosen a
fictional slave narrative which has never received the recognition that it deserves. It is a pioneer work of Afro-American
literature, the first significant novella by a Black writer in the
United States, and has remained little known since its initial
publication more than a century ago.

It was based on an actual slave revolt, aboard the ship *Creole*
carrying slaves down the Mississippi in 1841, which was successfully led by Madison Washington. The ship was prevented
from landing at New Orleans and arrived at Nassau, where the
former slaves were declared free by the British authorities after
a campaign waged by British abolitionists.

This novella was published in *Autographs for Freedom*, a
collection of anti-slavery writings edited on behalf of "The
Rochester Ladies' Anti-Slavery Society" to help raise funds for
Frederick Douglass's Paper, the weekly edited by Douglass as
a continuation of his earlier newspaper *The North Star*. The
book was published simultaneously in Boston and Cleveland, in
the United States, and in London, in 1853.

The Heroic Slave

PART I

> Oh! child of grief, why weepest thou?
> Why droops thy sad and mournful brow?
> Why is thy look so like despair?
> What deep, sad sorrow lingers there?

The State of Virginia is famous in American annals for the multitudinous array of her statesmen and heroes. She has been dignified by some the mother of statesmen. History has not been sparing in recording their names, or in blazoning their deeds. Her high position in this respect, has given her an enviable distinction among her sister States. With Virginia for his birth-place, even a man of ordinary parts, on account of the general partiality for her sons, easily rises to eminent stations. Men, not great enough to attract special attention in their native States, have, like a certain distinguished citizen in the State of New York, sighed and repined that they were not born in Virginia. Yet not all the great ones of the Old Dominion have, by the fact of their birthplace, escaped undeserved obscurity. By some strange neglect, *one* of the truest, manliest, and bravest of her children,—one who, in after years, will, I think, command the pen of genius to set his merits forth—holds now no higher place in the records of that grand old Commonwealth than is held by a horse or an ox. Let those account for it who can, but there stands the fact, that a man who loved liberty as well as did Patrick Henry— who deserved it as much as Thomas Jefferson—and who fought for it with a valor as high, an arm as strong, and against odds as great as he who led all the armies of the American colonies through the great war for freedom and independence, lives now only in the chattel records of his native state.

Glimpses of this great character are all that can now be presented. He is brought to view only by a few transient incidents and these afford but partial satisfaction. Like a guiding star on a stormy night, he is seen through the parted clouds and the howling tempests; or, like the gray peak of a menacing rock on a perilous coast, he is seen by the quivering flash of angry lightning, and he again disappears covered with mystery. Curiously, earnestly, anxiously we peer into the dark, and wish even for the blinding flash, or the light of northern skies to reveal him. But alas! he is still enveloped in darkness, and we return from the pursuit like a wearied and disheartened mother (after a tedious and unsuccessful search for a lost child), who returns weighed down with disappointment and sorrow. Speaking of marks, traces, possibles, and probabilities, we come before our readers.

In the spring of 1835, on a Sabbath morning, within hearing of the solemn peals of the church bells at a distant village, a Northern traveller through the State of Virginia drew up his horse to drink at a sparkling brook, near the edge of a dark pine forest. While his weary and thirsty steed drew in the grateful water, the rider caught the sound of a human voice, apparently engaged in earnest conversation.

Following the direction of the sound, he descried, among the tall pines, the man whose voice had arrested his attention. "To whom can he be speaking?" thought the traveller. "He seems to be alone." The circumstance interested him much, and he became intensely curious to know what thoughts and feelings, or, it might be, high aspirations, guided those rich and mellow accents. Tieing his horse at a short distance from the brook, he stealthily drew near the solitary speaker; and, concealing himself by the side of a huge fallen tree, he distinctly heard the following soliloquy:—

"What, then, is life to me? it is aimless and worthless, and worse than worthless. Those birds, perched on you swinging boughs, in friendly conclave, sounding forth their merry notes in seeming worship of the rising sun, though liable to the sportsman's fowling-piece, are still my superiors. They *live free*, though they may die slaves. They fly where they list by day, and retire in freedom at night. But what is freedom to me, or I to it? I am a *slave*,—born a slave, an abject slave,—even before I made part of this breathing world, and scourge was platted for my back; the fetters were forged for my limbs. How mean a thing am I. That accursed and crawling snake, that miserable reptile, that has just glided into its slimy home, is freer and better off than I. He escaped my blow, and is safe. But here am I, a man,—yes, *a man!*—with thoughts and wishes, with powers and faculties as far as angel's flight above that hated reptile,—yet he is my superior, and scorns to own me as his master, or to stop to take my blows. When he saw my uplifted arm, he darted beyond my reach, and turned to give me battle. I dare not do as much as that. I neither run nor fight, but do meanly stand, answering each heavy blow of a cruel master with doleful wails and piteous cries. I am galled with irons; but even these are more tolerable than the consciousness, the *galling* consciousness of cowardice and indecision. Can it be that I *dare* not run away? *Perish the thought,* I *dare* do any thing which may be done by another. When that young man struggled with the waves *for life,* and others stood back appalled in helpless horror, did I not plunge in, forgetful of life, to save his? The raging bull from whom all others fled, pale with fright, did I not keep at bay with a single pitchfork? Could a coward do that? *No,—no,—*I wrong myself,— I am no coward. *Liberty* I will have, or die in the attempt to gain it. This working that others may live in idleness! This cringing submission to insolence and curses! This living under the constant dread and apprehension of being sold and transferred, like a mere brute, is *too* much for me. I will stand it no longer. What others have done, I will do. These trusty legs, or these sinewy arms shall place me among the free. Tom escaped; so can I. The North Star will not be less kind to me

ANTI-SLAVE-CATCHERS'
MASS
CONVENTION!

All the People of this State, who are opposed to being made SLAVES or SLAVE-CATCHERS, and to having the Free Soil of Wisconsin made the hunting-ground for *Human Kidnappers*, and all who are willing to unite in a

☞STATE LEAGUE,🖘

to defend our State Sovereignty, our State Courts, and our State and National Constitutions, against the flagrant usurpations of U. S. Judges, Commissioners, and Marshals, and their Attorneys; and to maintain inviolate those great Constitutional Safeguards of Freedom—the WRIT OF HABEAS CORPUS, and the RIGHT OF TRIAL BY JURY—as old and sacred as Constitutional Liberty itself; and all who are willing to sustain the cause of those who are prosecuted, and to be prosecuted in Wisconsin, by the agents and executors of the Kidnapping Act of 1850, for the alleged crime of rescuing a human being from the hands of kidnappers, and restoring him to himself and to Freedom, are invited to meet at

18 A harsher fugitive slave law was passed by Congress in 1850, further endangering runaway slaves living in the North. It was fought by the militant anti-slavery forces, as this Wisconsin poster shows

than to him. I will follow it. I will at least make the trial. I have nothing to lose. If I am caught, I shall only be a slave. If I am shot, I shall only lose a life which is a burden and a curse. If I get clear, (as something tells me I shall,) liberty, the inalienable birth-right of every man, precious and price-less, will be mine. My resolution is fixed. *I shall be free."*

At these words the traveller raised his head cautiously and noiselessly, and caught, from his hiding place a full view of the unsuspecting speaker. Madison (for that was the name of our hero) was standing erect, a smile of satisfaction rippled upon his expressive countenance, like that which plays upon the face of one who has but just solved a difficult problem, or vanquished a malignant foe for at that moment he was free, at least in spirit. The future gleamed brightly before him, and his fetters lay broken at his feet. His air was triumphant.

Madison was of manly form. Tall, symmetrical, round, and strong. In his movements he seemed to combine, with the strength of the lion, a lion's elasticity. His torn sleeves dis-closed arms like polished iron. His face was "black, but comely." His eye, lit with emotion, kept guard under a brow as dark and as glossy as the raven's wing. His whole appear-ance betokened Herculean strength; yet there was nothing savage or forbidding in his aspect. A child might play in his arms, or dance on his shoulders. A giant's strength, but not a giant's heart was in him. His broad mouth and nose spoke only of good nature and kindness. But his voice, that unfailing index of the soul, though full and melodious, had that in it which could terrify as well as charm. He was just the man you would choose when hardships were to be endured, or danger to be encountered—intelligent and brave. He had the head to conceive, and the hand to execute. In a word, he was one to be sought as a friend, but to be dreaded as an enemy.

As our traveller gazed upon him, he almost trembled at the thought of his dangerous intrusion. Still he could not quit the place. He had long desired to sound the mysterious depths of the thoughts and feelings of a slave. He was not, therefore, disposed to allow so providential an opportunity to pass unimproved. He resolved to hear more; so he listened again for those mellow and mournful accents which, he says, made such an impression upon him as can never be erased. He did not have to wait long. There came another gush from the same full fountain; now bitter, and now sweet. Scathing denunciations of the cruelty and injustice of slavery; heart-touching narrations of his own personal suffering, intermingled with prayers to the God of the oppressed for help and deliverance, were followed by presentations of the dangers and difficulties of escape, and formed the burden of his eloquent utterances; but his high resolution clung to him,—for he ended each speech by an emphatic declaration of his purpose to be free. It seemed that the very repetition of this, imparted a glow to his countenance. The hope of freedom seemed to sweeten, for a season, the bitter cup of slavery, and to make it, for a time, tolerable; for when in the very whirlwind of anguish,—when his heart's cord seemed screwed up to snapping tension,—hope sprung up and soothed his troubled spirit. Fitfully he would exclaim, "How can I leave her? Poor thing! what can she do when I am gone? Oh! Oh! 'tis impossible that I can leave poor Susan!"

A brief pause intervened. Our traveller raised his head, and saw again the sorrow-smitten slave. His eye was fixed upon the ground. The strong man staggered under a heavy load. Recovering himself, he argued thus aloud: "All is uncertain here. To-morrow's sun may not rise before I am sold, and separated from her I love. What, then, could I do for her? I should be in more hopeless slavery, and she no nearer to liberty,—whereas if I were free,—my arms my own,—I might devise the means to rescue her."

This said, Madison cast around a searching glance, as if the thought of being overheard had flashed across his mind. He said no more, but, with measured steps, walked away, and was lost to the eye of our traveller amidst the wildering woods.

Long after Madison had left the ground, Mr. Listwell, (our traveller) remained in motionless silence, meditating on the extraordinary revelations to which he had listened. He seemed fastened to the spot, and stood half hoping, half fearing the return of the sable preacher to his solitary temple. The speech of Madison rung through the chambers of his soul, and vibrated through his entire frame. "Here is indeed a man," thought he, "of rare endowments,—a child of God,—guilty of no crime but the color of his skin,—hiding away from the face of humanity, and pouring out his thoughts and feelings, his hopes and resolutions to the lonely woods; to him those distant church bells have no grateful music. He shuns the church, the altar, and the great congregation of Christian worshippers, and wanders away to the gloomy forest, to utter in the vacant air complaints and griefs, which the religion of his times and his country can neither console nor relieve. Goaded almost to madness by the sense of the injustice done him, he resorts hither to give vent to his pent up feelings, and to debate with himself the feasibility of plans, plans of his own invention, for his own deliverance. From this hour I am an abolitionist. I have seen enough and heard enough, and I shall go to my home in Ohio resolved to atone for my past indifference to this ill-starred race, by making such exertions as I shall be able to do, for the speedy emancipation of every slave in the land.

PART II

"The gaudy, blabbling and remorseful day
Is crept into the bosom of the sea;
And now loud-howling wolves arouse the jades
That drag the tragic melancholy night;

Who with their drowsy, slow, and flagging wings
Clip dead men's graves, and from their misty jaws
Breathe foul contagious darkness in the air."
                    Shakespeare

Five years after the foregoing singular occurrence, in the winter of 1840, Mr. and Mrs. Listwell sat together by the fireside of their own happy home, in the State of Ohio. The children were all gone to bed. A single lamp burnt brightly on the centretable. All was still and comfortable within; but the night was cold and dark; a heavy wind sighed and moaned sorrowfully around the house and barn, occasionally bringing against the clattering windows a stray leaf from the large oak trees that embowered their dwelling. It was a night for strange noises and for strange fancies. A whole wilderness of thought might pass through one's mind during such an evening. The smouldering embers, partaking of the spirit of the restless night, became fruitful of varied and fantastic pictures, and revived many bygone scenes and old impressions. The happy pair seemed to sit in silent fascination, gazing on the fire. Suddenly this *reverie* was interrupted by a heavy growl. Ordinarily such an occurrence would have scarcely provoked a single word, or excited the least apprehension. But there are certain seasons when the slightest sound sends a jar through all the subtle chambers of the mind; and such a season was this. The happy pair started up, as if some sudden danger had come upon them. The growl was from their trusty watchdog.

"What can it mean? certainly no one can be out on such a night as this," said Mrs. Listwell.

"The wind has deceived the dog, my dear; he has mistaken the noise of falling branches, brought down by the wind, for that of the footsteps of persons coming to the house. I have several times to-night thought that I heard the sound of footsteps. I am sure, however, that it was but the wind. Friends would not be likely to come out at such an hour, or such a night; and thieves are too lazy and self-indulgent to expose themselves to this biting frost; but should there be anyone about, our brave old Monte, who is on the lookout, will not be slow in sounding the alarm."

Saying this they quietly left the window, wither they had gone to learn the cause of the menacing growl, and re-seated themselves by the fire, as if reluctant to leave the slowly expiring embers, although the hour was late. A few minutes only intervened after resuming their seats, when again their sober meditations were disturbed. Their faithful dog now growled and barked furiously, as if assailed by an advancing foe. Simultaneously the good couple arose, and stood in mute expectation. The contest without seemed fierce and violent. It was, however, soon over,—the barking ceased, for, with true canine instinct, Monte quickly discovered that a friend, not an enemy of the family, was coming to the house, and instead of rushing to repel the supposed intruder, he was now at the door, whimpering and dancing for the admission of himself and his newly made friend.

Mr. Listwell knew by this movement that all was well; he advanced and opened the door, and saw by the light that streamed out into the darkness, a tall man advancing slowly towards the house, with a stick in one hand, and a small bundle in the other. "It is a traveller," thought he, "who has missed his way, and is coming to inquire the road. I am glad we did not go to bed earlier,—I have felt all the evening as if somebody would be here to-night."

The man had now halted a short distance from the door, and looked prepared alike for flight or battle. "Come in, sir, don't be alarmed, you have probably lost your way."

Slightly hesitating, the traveller walked in; not, however, without regarding his host with a scrutinizing glance. "No, sir," said he "I have come to ask you a greater favor."

Instantly Mr. Listwell exclaimed, (as the recollection of

the Virginia forest scene flashed upon him,) "Oh, sir, I know not your name, but I have seen your face, and heard your voice before. I am glad to see you. *I know all.* You are flying for your liberty,—be seated,—be seated,—banish all fear. You are safe under my roof."

This recognition, so unexpected, rather disconcerted and disquieted the noble fugitive. The timidity and suspicion of persons escaping from slavery are easily awakened, and often what is intended to dispel the one, and to allay the other, has precisely the opposite effect. It was so in this case. Quickly observing the unhappy impression made by his words and action, Mr. Listwell assumed a more quiet and inquiring aspect, and finally succeeded in removing the apprehensions which his very natural and generous salutation had aroused.

Thus assured, the stranger said, "Sir, you have rightly guessed, I am, indeed, a fugitive from slavery. My name is Madison,—Madison Washington my mother used to call me. I am on my way to Canada, where I learn that persons of my color are protected in all the rights of men; and my object in calling upon you was, to beg the privilege of resting my weary limbs for the night in your barn. It was my purpose to have continued my journey till morning; but the piercing cold, and the frowning darkness compelled me to seek shelter; and, seeing a light through the lattice of your window, I was encouraged to come here to beg the privilege named. You will do me a great favor by affording me shelter for the night."

"A resting-place, indeed, sir, you shall have; not, however, in my barn, but in the best room of my house. Consider yourself, if you please, under the roof of a friend; for such I am to you, and to all your deeply injured race."

While this introductory conversation was going on, the kind lady had revived the fire, and was diligently preparing supper; for she, not less than her husband, felt for the sorrows of the oppressed and hunted ones of earth, and was always glad of an opportunity to do them a service. A bountiful repast was quickly prepared, and the hungry and toil-worn bond-man was cordially invited to partake thereof. Gratefully he acknowledged the favor of his benevolent benefactress; but appeared scarcely to understand what such hospitality could mean. It was the first time in his life that he had met so humane and friendly a greeting at the hands of persons whose color was unlike his own; yet it was impossible for him to doubt the charitableness of his new friends, or the genuine-ness of the welcome so freely given; and he therefore, with many thanks, took his seat at the table with Mr. and Mrs. Listwell, who, desirous to make him feel at home, took a cup of tea themselves, while urging upon Madison the best that the house could afford.

Supper over, all doubts and apprehensions banished, the three drew around the blazing fire, and a conversation com-menced which lasted till long after midnight.

"Now," said Madison to Mr. Listwell, "I was a little sur-prised and alarmed when I came in, by what you said; do tell me, sir, *why* you thought you had seen my face before, and by what you knew me to be a fugitive from slavery; for I am sure that I never was before in this neighborhood, and I certainly sought to conceal what I supposed to be the man-ner of a fugitive slave."

Mr. Listwell at once frankly disclosed the secret; describing the place where he first saw him; rehearsing the language which he (Madison) had used; referring to the effect which his manner and speech had made upon him; declaring the resolution he there formed to be an abolitionist; telling how often he had spoken of the circumstance, and the deep con-cern he had ever since felt to know what had become of him; and whether he had carried out the purpose to make his escape, as in the woods he declared he would do.

"Ever since that morning," said Mr. Listwell, "you have seldom been absent from my mind, and though now I did not dare to hope that I should ever see you again, I have often wished that such might be my fortune; for, from that hour, your face seemed to be daguerreotyped on my memory."

Madison looked quite astonished, and felt amazed at the narration to which he had listened. After recovering himself he said, "I well remember that morning, and the bitter anguish that wrung my heart; I will state the occasion of it. I had, on the previous Saturday, suffered a cruel lashing; had been tied up to the limb of a tree, with my feet chained together, and a heavy iron bar placed between my ankles. Thus suspended, I received on my naked back forty stripes, and was kept in this distressing position three or four hours, and was then let down, only to have my torture increased; for my bleeding back, gashed by the cow-skin, was washed by the overseer with old brine, partly to augment my suffering, and partly, as he said, to prevent inflammation. My crime was that I had stayed longer at the mill, the day previous, than it was thought I ought to have done, which, I assured my master and the overseer, was no fault of mine; but no excuses were allowed. 'Hold your tongue, you impudent rascal,' met my every explanation. Slave-holders are so imperious when their passions are excited, as to construe every word of the slave into insolence. I could do nothing but submit to the agonizing infliction. Smarting still from the wounds, as well as from the consciousness of being whipt for no cause, I took advantage of the absence of my master, who had gone to church, to spend the time in the woods, and brood over my wretched lot. Oh, sir, I remember it well,—and can never forget it."

"But this was five years ago; where have you been since?"

"I will try to tell you," said Madison, "Just four weeks after that Sabbath morning, I gathered up the few rags of clothing I had, and started, as I supposed, for the North and for freedom. I must not stop to describe my feelings on taking this step. It seemed like taking a leap into the dark. The thought of leaving my poor wife and two little children caused me indescribable anguish; but consoling myself with the reflection that once free, I could, possibly, devise ways and means to gain their freedom also, I nerved myself up to make the attempt. I started, but ill-luck attended me; for after being out a whole week, strange to say, I still found myself on my master's grounds; the third night after being out, a season of clouds and rain set in, wholly preventing me from seeing the North Star, which I had trusted as my guide, not dreaming that clouds might intervene between us.

"This circumstance was fatal to my project, for in losing my star, I lost my way; so when I supposed I was far towards the North, and had almost gained my freedom, I discovered myself at the very point from which I had started. It was a severe trial, for I arrived at home in great destitution; my feet were sore, and in travelling in the dark, I had dashed my foot against a stump, and started a nail, and lamed myself. I was wet and cold; one week had exhausted all my stores; and when I landed on my master's plantation, with all my work to do over again,—hungry, tired, lame, and bewildered,—I almost cursed the day that I was born. In this extremity I approached the quarters. I did so stealthily, although in my desperation I hardly cared whether I was discovered or not. Peeping through the rents of the quarters, I saw my fellow-slaves seated by a warm fire, merrily passing away the time, as though their hearts knew no sorrow. Although I envied their seeming contentment, all wretched as I was, I despised the cowardly acquiescence in their own degradation which it implied, and felt a kind of pride and glory in my own desperate lot. I dared not enter the quarters,—for where there is seeming contentment with slavery, there is certain treachery to freedom. I proceeded towards the great house, in the hope of catching a glimpse of my poor wife, whom I knew might be trusted with my secrets even on the scaffold. Just as I reached the fence which divided the field from the garden, I saw a woman in the yard, who in the darkness I took to be my wife; but a nearer approach told me it was not she. I was

about to speak; had I done so, I would not have been here
this night; for an alarm would have been sounded, and the
hunters been put on my track. Here were hunger, cold, thirst,
disappointment, and chagrin, confronted only by the dim hope
of liberty. I tremble to think of that dreadful hour. To face
the deadly cannon's mouth in warm blood unterrified, is, I
think, a small achievement, compared with a conflict like this
with gaunt starvation. The gnawings of hunger conquer by
degrees, till all that a man has he would give in exchange for
a single crust of bread. Thank God, I was not quite reduced
to this extremity.

"Happily for me, before the fatal moment of utter despair,
my good wife made her appearance in the yard. It was she;
I knew her step. All was well now. I was, however, afraid
to speak, lest I should frighten her. Yet speak I did; and, to
my great joy, my voice was known. Our meeting can be more
easily imagined than described. For a time hunger, thirst,
weariness, and lameness were forgotten. But it was soon necessary for her to return to the house. She being a house-
servant, her absence from the kitchen, if discovered, might
have excited suspicion. Our parting was like tearing the flesh
from my bones; yet it was the part of wisdom for her to go.
She left me with the purpose of meeting me at midnight in
the very forest where you last saw me. She knew the place
well, as one of my melancholy resorts, and could easily find
it, though the night was dark.

"I hastened away, therefore, and concealed myself, to
await the arrival of my good angel. As I lay there among the
leaves, I was strongly tempted to return again to the house
of my master and give myself up; but remembering my solemn
pledge on that memorable Sunday morning, I was able to
linger out the two long hours between ten and midnight. I
may well call them long hours. I have endured much hard-
ship; I have encountered many perils; but the anxiety of those
two hours, was the bitterest I ever experienced. True to her

word, my wife came laden with provisions, and we sat down on the side of a log, at that dark and lonesome hour of the night. I cannot say we talked; our feelings were too great for that; yet we came to an understanding that I should make the woods my home, for if I gave myself up, I should be whipped and sold away; and if I started for the North, I should leave a wife doubly dear to me. We mutually determined, therefore, that I should remain in the vicinity. In the dismal swamps I lived, sir, five long years,—a cave for my home during the day. I wandered about at night with the wolf and the bear,—sustained by the promise that my good Susan would meet me in the pine woods at least once a week. This promise was redeemed, I assure you, to the letter, greatly to my relief. I had partly become contented with my mode of life, and had made up my mind to spend my days there; but the wilderness that sheltered me thus long took fire, and refused longer to be my hiding-place.

"I will not harrow up your feelings by portraying the terrific scene of this awful conflagration. There is nothing to which I can liken it. It was horribly and indescribably grand. The whole world seemed on fire, and it appeared to me that the day of judgment had come; that the burning bowels of the earth had burst forth, and that the end of all things was at hand. Bears and wolves, scorched from their mysterious hiding-places in the earth, and all the wild inhabitants of the untrodden forest, filled with a common dismay, ran forth, yelling, howling, bewildered amidst the smoke and flame. The very heavens seemed to rain down fire through the towering trees; it was by the merest chance that I escaped the devouring element. Running before it, and stopping occasionally to take breath, I looked back to behold its frightful ravages, and to drink in its savage magnificence. It was awful, thrilling, solemn, beyond compare. When aided by the fitful wind, the merciless tempest of fire swept on, sparkling, creaking, cracking, curling, roaring, out-doing in its dreadful splendor a thousand thunderstorms at once. From tree to tree it leaped, swallowing them up in its lurid, baleful glare; and leaving them leafless, limbless, charred, and lifeless behind. The scene was overwhelming, stunning,—nothing was spared,—cattle, tame and wild, herds of swine and of deer, wild beasts of every name and kind,—huge night-birds, bats, and owls, that had retired to their homes in lofty tree-tops to rest, perished in that fiery storm. The long-winged buzzard and croaking raven mingled their dismal cries with those of the countless myriads of small birds that rose up to the skies, and were lost to the sight in clouds of smoke and flame. Oh, I shudder when I think of it! Many a poor wandering fugitive, who, like myself, had sought among wild beasts the mercy denied by our fellow men, saw, in helpless consternation, his dwelling-place and city of refuge reduced to ashes forever. It was this grand conflagration that drove me hither; I ran alike from fire and from slavery."

After a slight pause, (for both speaker and hearers were deeply moved by the above recital,) Mr. Listwell, addressing Madison, said, "If it does not weary you too much, do tell us something of your journeyings since this disastrous burning,— we are deeply interested in everything which can throw light on the hardships of persons escaping from slavery; we could hear you talk all night; are there no incidents that you could relate of your travels hither? or are they such that you do not like to mention them?"

"For the most part, sir, my course has been uninterrupted; and, considering the circumstances, at times even pleasant. I have suffered little for want of food; but I need not tell you how I got it. Your moral code may differ from mine, as your customs and usages are different. The fact is, sir, during my flight, I felt myself robbed by society of all my just rights; that I was in an enemy's land, who sought both my life and my liberty. They had transformed me into a brute; made merchandise of my body, and, for all the purposes of my

flight, turned day into night,—and guided by my own necessities, and in contempt of their conventionalities, I did not
scruple to take bread where I could get it."

"And just there you were right," said Mr. Listwell; "I once
had doubts on this point myself, but a conversation with Ger-
rit Smith, (a man, by the way, that I wish you could see, for
he is a devoted friend of your race, and I know he would
receive you gladly,) put an end to all my doubts on this point.
But do not let me interrupt you."

"I had but one narrow escape during my whole journey,"
said Madison.

"Do let us hear of it," said Mr. Listwell.

"Two weeks ago," continued Madison, "after travelling
all night, I was overtaken by daybreak, in what seemed to
me an almost interminable wood. I deemed it unsafe to go
farther, and, as usual, I looked around for a suitable tree in
which to spend the day. I liked one with a bushy top, and
found one just to my mind. Up I climbed, and hiding myself
as well as I could, I, with this strap, (pulling one out of his
old coat-pocket,) lashed myself to a bough, and flattered
myself that I should get a *good night's* sleep that day; but in
this I was soon disappointed. I had scarcely got fastened to
my natural hammock, when I heard the voices of a number
of persons, apparently approaching the part of the woods
where I was. Upon my word, sir, I dreaded more these human
voices than I should have done those of wild beasts. I was at
a loss to know what to do. If I descended, I should probably
be discovered by the men; and if they had dogs I should,
doubtless, be '*treed.*' It was an anxious moment, but hardships
and dangers have been the accompaniments of my life; and
have, perhaps, imparted to me a certain hardness of character,
which, to some extent, adapts me to them. In my present pre-
dicament, I decided to hold my place in the tree-top and abide
the consequences. But here I must disappoint you; for the
men, who were all colored, halted at least a hundred yards

from me, and began with their axes, in right good earnest, to
attack the trees. The sound of their laughing axes was like
the report of as many well-charged pistols. By and by there
came down at least a dozen trees with a terrible crash. They
leaped upon the fallen trees with an air of victory. I could
see no dog with them, and felt myself comparatively safe,
though I could not forget the possibility that some freak or
fancy might bring the axe a little nearer my dwelling than
comported with my safety.

"There was no sleep for me that day, and I wished for
night. You may imagine that the thought of having the tree
attacked under me was far from agreeable, and that it very
easily kept me on the look-out. The day was not without
diversion. The men at work semed to be a gay set; and they
would often make the woods resound with that uncontrolled
laughter for which we, as a race, are remarkable. I held my
place in the tree till sunset,—saw the men put on their jackets
to be off. I observed that all left the ground except one, whom
I saw sitting on the side of a stump, with his head bowed,
and his eyes apparently fixed on the ground. I became interested in him. After sitting in the position to which I have
alluded ten or fifteen minutes, he left the stump, walked
directly towards the tree in which I was secreted, and halted
almost under the same. He stood for a moment and looked
around, deliberately and reverently took off his hat, by which
I saw that he was a man in the evening of life, slightly bald
and quite gray. After laying down his hat carefully, he knelt
and prayed aloud, and such a prayer, the most fervent,
earnest, and solemn, to which I think I ever listened. After
reverently addressing the Almighty, as the all-wise, all-good,
and the common Father of all mankind, he besought God for
grace, for strength, to bear up under, and to endure, as a good
soldier, all the hardships and trials which beset the journey
of life, and to enable him to live in a manner which accorded
with the gospel of Christ. His soul now broke out in humble

CAUTION!!

COLORED PEOPLE

OF BOSTON, ONE & ALL,

You are hereby respectfully CAUTIONED and advised, to avoid conversing with the

Watchmen and Police Officers of Boston,

For since the recent ORDER OF THE MAYOR & ALDERMEN, they are empowered to act as

KIDNAPPERS

AND

Slave Catchers,

And they have already been actually employed in KIDNAPPING, CATCHING, AND KEEPING SLAVES. Therefore, if you value your LIBERTY, and the *Welfare of the Fugitives* among you, *Shun* them in every possible manner, as so many *HOUNDS* on the track of the most unfortunate of your race.

Keep a Sharp Look Out for KIDNAPPERS, and have TOP EYE open.

APRIL 24, 1851.

19 After the passage of the Fugitive Slave Act of 1850 the anti-slavery forces issued posters warning Black people of the intense activities of the police in the North. Thousands of runaways went on to Canada for safety.

supplication for deliverance from bondage. 'O thou,' said he, 'that hearest the raven's cry, take pity on poor me! O deliver me! O deliver me! in mercy, O God, deliver me from the chains and manifold hardships of slavery! With thee, O Father, all things are possible. Thou canst stand and measure the earth. Thou has beheld and drove asunder the nations,— all power is in thy hand,—thou didst say of old, "I have seen the affliction of my people, and am come to deliver them,"— Oh look down upon our afflictions, and have mercy upon us.' But I cannot repeat his prayer, nor can I give you an idea of its deep pathos. I had given but little attention to religion, and had but little faith in it; yet as the old man prayed, I felt almost like coming down and kneel by his side, and mingle my broken complaint with his.

"He had already gained my confidence; as how could it be otherwise? I knew enough of religion to know that the man who prays in secret is far more likely to be sincere than he who loves to pray standing in the street, or in the great congregation. When he arose from his knees, like another Zacheus, I came down from the tree. He seemed a little alarmed at first, but I told him my story, and the good man embraced me in his arms, and assured me of his sympathy.

"I was now about out of provisions, and thought I might safely ask him to help me replenish my store. He said he had no money; but if he had, he would freely give it me. I told him I had *one dollar;* it was all the money I had in the world. I gave it to him, and asked him to purchase some crackers and cheese, and to kindly bring me the balance; that I would remain in or near that place, and would come to him on his return, if he would whistle. He was gone only about an hour. Meanwhile, from some cause or other, I know not what, (but as you shall see very wisely,) I changed my place. On his return I started to meet him; but it seemed as if the shadow of approaching danger fell upon my spirit, and checked my progress. In a very few minutes, closely on the heels of the old man, I distinctly saw *fourteen men*, with something like guns in their hands."

"Oh! the old wretch!" exclaimed Mrs. Listwell "he had betrayed you, had he?"

"I think not," said Madison, "I cannot believe that the old man was to blame. He probably went into a store, asked for the article for which I sent, and presented the bill I gave him; and it is so unusual for slaves in the county to have money, that fact, doubtless, excited suspicion, and gave rise to inquiry. I can easily believe that the truthfulness of the old man's character compelled him to disclose the facts; and thus were these blood-thirsty men put on my track. Of course I did not present myself; but hugged my hiding-place securely. If discovered and attacked, I resolved to sell my life as dearly as possibly.

"After searching about the woods silently for a time, the whole company gathered around the old man; one charged him with lying, and called him an old villain; said he was a thief; charged him with stealing money; said if he did not instantly tell where he got it, they would take the shirt from his old back, and give him thirty-nine lashes.

" 'I did *not* steal the money,' said the old man, 'it was given me, as I told you at the store; and if the man who gave it me is not here, it is not my fault.'

" 'Hush! you lying old rascal; we'll make you smart for it. You shall not leave this spot until you have told where you got that money.'

"They now took hold of him, and began to strip him; while others went to get sticks with which to beat him. I felt, at the moment, like rushing out in the midst of them; but considering that the old man would be whipped the more for having aided a fugitive slave, and that, perhaps, in the *melée* he might be killed outright, I disobeyed this impulse. They tied him to a tree, and began to whip him. My own flesh crept at every blow, and I seem to hear the old man's piteous cries even now. They laid thirty-nine lashes on his bare back, and were going to repeat that number, when one of the company besought his comrades to desist. 'You'll kill the d——d old scoundrel! You've already whipt a dollar's worth out of him, even if he stole it!' 'O yes,' said another, 'let him down. He'll never tell us another lie, I'll warrant ye!' With this one of the company untied the old man, and bid him go about his business.

The old man left, but the company remained as much as an hour, scouring the woods. Round and round they went, turning up the underbrush, and peering about like so many bloodhounds. Two or three times they came within six feet of where I lay. I tell you I held my stick with a firmer grasp than I did in coming up to your house tonight. I expected to level one of them at least. Fortunately, however, I eluded their pursuit, and they left me alone in the woods.

My last dollar was now gone, and you may well suppose I felt the loss of it; but the thought of being once again free to pursue my journey, prevented that depression which a sense of destitution causes; so swinging my little bundle on my back, I caught a glimpse of the *Great Bear* (which ever points the way to my beloved star,) and I started again on my journey. What I lost in money I made up at a hen-roost that same night, upon which I fortunately came."

"But you didn't eat your food raw? How did you cook it?" said Mrs. Listwell.

"O no, Madam," said Madison, turning to his little bundle; —"I had the means of cooking." Here he took out of his bundle an old-fashioned tinder-box, and taking up a piece of a file, which he brought with him, he struck it with a heavy flint, and brought out at least a dozen sparks at once. "I have had this old box," said he, "more than five years. It is the *only* property saved from the fire in the dismal swamp. It has done me good service. It had given me the means of broiling many a chicken!"

It seemed quite a relief to Mrs. Listwell to know that

Madison had, at least, lived upon cooked food. Women have a perfect horror of eating uncooked food.

By this time thoughts of what was best to be done about getting Madison to Canada, began to trouble Mr. Listwell; for the laws of Ohio were very stringent against any one who should aid, or who were found aiding a slave to escape through that State. A citizen, for the simple act of taking a fugitive slave in his carriage, had just been stripped of all his property, and thrown penniless upon the world. Notwithstanding this, Mr. Listwell was determined to see Madison safely on his way to Canada. "Give yourself no uneasiness," said he to Madison, "for if it cost my farm, I shall see you safely out of the States, and on your way to a land of liberty. Thank God that there is *such* a land so near us! You will spend to-morrow with us, and to-morrow night I will take you in my carriage to the Lake. Once upon that, and you are safe."

"Thank you! thank you,!" said the fugitive; "I will commit myself to your care."

For the *first* time during *five* years, Madison enjoyed the luxury of resting his limbs on a comfortable bed, and inside a human habitation. Looking at the white sheets, he said to Mr. Listwell, "What sir! you don't mean that I shall sleep in that bed?"

"Oh yes, oh yes."

After Mr. Listwell left the room, Madison said he really hesitated whether or not he should lie on the floor; for that was *far* more comfortable and inviting than any bed to which he had been used.

We pass over the thoughts and feelings, the hopes and fears, the plans and purposes, that revolved in the mind of Madison during the day that he was secreted at the house of Mr. Listwell. The reader will be content to know that nothing occurred to endanger his liberty, or to excite alarm. Many were the little attentions bestowed upon him in his quiet retreat and hiding-place. In the evening, Mr. Listwell, after treating Madison to a new suit of winter clothes, and replenishing his exhausted purse with five dollars, all in silver, brought out his two-horse wagon, well provided with buffaloes, and silently started off with him to Cleveland. They arrived there without interruption, a few minutes before sunrise the next morning. Fortunately the steamer Admiral lay at the wharf, and was to start for Canada at nine o'clock. Here the last anticipated danger was surmounted. It was feared that just at this point the hunters of men might be on the look-out, and, possibly, pounce upon their victim. Mr. Listwell saw the captain of the boat; cautiously sounded him on the matter of carrying liberty-loving passengers, before he introduced his precious charge. This done, Madison was conducted on board. With usual generosity this true subject of the emancipation queen welcomed Madison, and assured him that he should be safely landed in Canada, free of charge. Madison now felt himself no more a piece of merchandise, but a passenger, and, like any other passenger, going about his business, carrying with him what belonged to him, and nothing which rightfully belonged to anybody else.

Wrapped in his new winter suit, snug and comfortable, a pocket full of silver, safe from his pursuers, embarked for a free country, Madison gave every sign of sincere gratitude, and bade his kind benefactor farewell, with such a grip of the hand as bespoke a heart full of honest manliness, and a soul that knew how to appreciate kindness. It need scarcely be said that Mr. Listwell was deeply moved by the gratitude and friendship he had excited in a nature so noble as that of the fugitive. He went to his home that day with a joy and gratification which knew no bounds. He had done something "to deliver the spoiled out of the hands of the spoiler," he had given bread to the hungry, and clothes to the naked; he had befriended a man to whom the laws of his country forbade all friendship,—and in proportion to the odds against his righteous deed, was the delightful satisfaction that gladdened his heart. On reaching home, he exclaimed, *"He is safe, —he is safe,—he is safe,"*—and the cup of his joy was shared by his excellent lady. The following letter was received from Madison a few days after.

"Windsor, Canada West, Dec. 16, 1840.

My dear Friend,—for such you truly are:—

Madison is out of the woods at last; I nestle in the mane of the British lion, protected by his mighty paw from the talons and the beak of the American eagle. I AM FREE, and breathe an atmosphere too pure for *slaves,* slave-hunters, or slave-holders. My heart is full. As many thanks to you, sir, and to your kind lady, as there are pebbles on the shores of Lake Erie; and may the blessing of God rest upon you both. You will never be forgotten by your profoundly grateful friend,

MADISON WASHINGTON."

PART III

————His head was with his heart,
And that was far away!
Childe Harold.

Just upon the edge of the great road from Petersburg, Virginia, to Richmond, and only about fifteen miles from the latter place, there stands a somewhat ancient and famous tavern, quite notorious in its better days, as being the grand resort for most of the leading gamblers, horse-racers, cock-fighters, and slave-traders from all the country round about. This old rookery, the nucleus of all sorts of birds, mostly those of ill omen, has, like everything else peculiar to Virginia, lost much of its ancient consequence and splendor; yet it keeps up some appearance of gaiety and high life, and is still frequented, even by respectable travellers, who are unacquainted with its past history and present condition. Its fine old portico looks well at a distance, and gives the building an air of grandeur. A nearer view, however, does little to sustain this pretension. The house is large, and its style imposing, but time and dissipation, unfailing in their results, have made ineffaceable marks upon it, and it must, in the common course of events, soon be numbered with the things that were. The gloomy mantle of ruin is, already, outspread to envelop it, and its remains even but now remind one of a human skull, after the flesh has mingled with the earth. Old hats and rags fill the places in the upper windows once occupied by large panes of glass, and the moulding boards along the roofing have dropped off from their places, leaving holes and crevices in the rented wall for bats and swallows to build their nests in. The platform of the portico, which fronts the highway is a rickety affair, its planks are loose, and in some places entirely gone, leaving effective mantraps in their stead for nocturnal ramblers. The wooden pillars, which once supported it, but which now hang as encumbrances, are all rotten, and tremble with the touch. A part of the stable, a fine old structure in its day, which has given comfortable shelter to hundreds of the noblest steeds of "the Old Dominion" at once, was blown down many years ago, and never has been, and probably never will be rebuilt. The doors of the barn are in wretched condition; they will shut with a little human strength to help their worn out hinges, but not otherwise. The side of the great building seen from the road is much discolored in sundry places by slops poured from the upper windows, rendering it unsightly ,and offensive in other respects. Three or four great dogs, looking as dull and gloomy as the mansion itself, lie stretched out along the doorsills under the portico; and double the number of loafers, some of them completely rum-ripe, and others ripening, dispose themselves like so many sentinels about the front of the house. These latter understand the science of scraping acquaintance to perfection. They know every-body, and almost every-body knows them. Of course, as their title implies they have no regular employment. They are (to use an expressive phrase) *hangers on,* or still better, they are what sailors would denominate *holders-on to the slack, in everybody's mess, and in nobody's watch.* They are, however, as good as the newspaper for the events of the day, and they sell their knowledge almost as cheap. Money they seldom have; yet they always have capital the most reliable. They make their way with a succeeding traveller by intelligence gained from a preceding one. All the great names of Virginia they know by heart, and have seen their owners often. The history of the house is folded in their lips, and they rattle off stories in connection with it, equal to the guides at Dryburgh Abbey. He must be a shrewd man, and well skilled in the art of evasion, who gets out of the hands of these fellows without being at the expense of a treat.

It was at this old tavern, while on a second visit to the State of Virginia in 1841, that Mr. Listwell, unacquainted with the fame of the place, turned aside, about sunset, to pass the night. Riding up to the house, he had scarcely dismounted, when one of the half dozen bar-room fraternity met and addressed him in a manner exceedingly bland. and accommodating.

"Fine evening, sir."

"Very fine," said Mr. Listwell. "This is a tavern, I believe?"

"O yes, sir, yes; although you may think it looks a little the worse for wear, it was once as good a house as any in Virginy. I make no doubt if ye spend the night here, you'll think it a good house yet; for there aint a more accommodating man in the country than you'll find the landlord."

Listwell. "The most I want is a good bed for myself, and

a full manger for my horse. If I get these, I shall be quite satisfied."

Loafer. "Well, I alloys like to hear a gentleman talk for his horse; and just because the horse can't talk for itself. A man that don't care about his beast, and don't look arter it when he's travelling, aint much in my eye anyhow. Now, sir, I likes a horse, and I'll guarantee your horse will be taken good care on here. That old stable, for all you see it looks so shabby now, once sheltered the great *Eclipse,* when he run here agin *Batchelor* and *Jumping Jemmy.* Them was fast horses, but he beat 'em both."

Listwell. "Indeed."

Loafer. "Well, I rather reckon you've travelled a right smart distance to-day, from the look of your horse?"

Listwell. "Forty miles only."

Loafer. "Well! I'll be darned if that aint a pretty good *only.* Mister, that beast of yours is a singed cat, I warrant you. I never see'd a creature like that that was'nt good on the road. You've come about forty miles, then?"

Listwell. "Yes, yes, and a pretty good pace at that."

Loafer. "You're somewhat in a hurry, then, I make no doubt? I reckon I could guess if I would, what you're going to Richmond for? It would'nt be much of a guess either; for it's rumored hereabouts, that there's to be the greatest sale of niggers at Richmond to-morrow that has taken place there in a long time; and I'll be bound you're a going there to have a hand in it."

Listwell. "Why, you must think, then, that there's money to be made at that business?"

Loafer. "Well, 'pon my honor, sir, I never made any that way myself; but it stands to reason that it's a money making business; for almost all other business in Virginia is dropped to engage in this. One thing is sartain, I never see'd a nigger-buyer yet that had'nt a plenty of money, and he was'nt as free with it as water. I has known one on 'em to treat as high as twenty times in a night; and, ginerally speaking, they's men of edication, and knows all about the government. The fact is, sir, I alloys like to hear 'em talk, bekase I alloys can learn something from them."

Listwell. "What may I call your name, sir?"

Loafer. "Well, now, they calls me Wilkes. I'm known all around by the gentlemen that comes here. They all knows old Wilkes."

Listwell. "Well, Wilkes, you seem to be acquainted here, and I see you have a strong liking for a horse. Be so good as to speak a kind word for mine to the hostler to-night, and you'll not lose anything by it."

Loafer. "Well, sir, I see you don't say much, but you've got an insight into things. It's alloys wise to get the good will of them that's acquainted about a tavern, for a man don't know when he goes into a house what may happen, or how much he may need a friend." Here the loafer gave Mr. Listwell a significant grin, which expressed a sort of triumphant pleasure at having, as he supposed, by his tact succeeded in placing so fine appearing a gentleman under obligations to him.

The pleasure, however, was mutual; for there was something so insinuating in the glance of this loquacious customer, that Mr. Listwell was very glad to get quit of him, and to do so more successfully, he ordered his supper to be brought to him in his private room, private to the eye, but not to the ear. This room was directly over the bar, and the plastering being off, nothing but pine boards and naked laths separated him from the disagreeable company below,—he could easily hear what was said in the bar-room, and was rather glad of the advantage it afforded, for, as you shall see, it furnished him important hints as to the manner and deportment he should assume during his stay at that tavern.

Mr. Listwell says he had got into his room but a few moments, when he heard the officious Wilkes below, in a tone of disappointment, exclaim, "Whar's that gentleman?" Wilkes was evidently expecting to meet with his friend at the bar-room, on his return, and had no doubt of his doing the handsome thing. "He has gone to his room," answered the landlord, "and has ordered his supper to be brought to him."

Here some one shouted out, "Who is he, Wilkes? Where's he going?"

"Well, now, I'll be hanged if I know; but I'm willing to make any man a bet of this old hat agin a five dollar bill, that that gent is as full of money as a dog is of fleas. He's going down to Richmond to buy niggers, I make no doubt. He's no fool, I warrant ye."

"Well, he act d——d strange," said another, "anyhow. I likes to see a man, when he comes up to a tavern, to come straight into the bar-room, and show that he's a man among men. Nobody was going to bite him."

"Now, I don't blame him a bit for not coming in here. That man knows his business, and means to take care on his money," answered Wilkes.

"Wilkes, you're a fool. You only say that, becase you hope to get a few coppers out on him."

"You only measure my corn by your half-bushel, I won't say that you're only mad becase I got the chance of speaking to him first."

"O Wilkes! you're known here. You'll praise up any body that will give you a copper; besides, 'tis my opinion that that fellow who took his long slab-sides up stairs, for all the world just like a half-scared woman, afraid to look honest men in the face, is a *Northerner,* and as mean as dishwater."

"Now what will you bet on that," said Wilkes.

The speaker said, "I make no bets with you, 'kase you can get that fellow up stairs there to say anything."

"Well," said Wilkes, "I am willing to bet any man in the company that *that* gentleman is a *nigger*-buyer. He did'nt tell me so right down, but I reckon I knows enough about men to give a pretty clean guess as to what they are arter."

The dispute as to *who* Mr. Listwell was, what his business, where he was going, etc., was kept up with much animation for some time, and more than once threatened a serious disturbance of the peace. Wilkes had his friends as well as his opponents. After this sharp debate, the company amused themselves by drinking whiskey, and telling stories. The latter consisting of quarrels, fights, *recontres,* and duels, in which distinguished persons of that neighborhood, and frequenters of that house, had been actors. Some of these stories were frightful enough, and were told, too, with a relish which bespoke the pleasure of the parties with the horrid scenes they portrayed. It would not be proper here to give the reader any idea of the vulgarity and dark profanity which rolled, as "a sweet morsel," under these corrupt tongues. A more brutal set of creatures, perhaps, never congregated.

Disgusted, and a little alarmed withal, Mr. Listwell, who was not accustomed to such entertainment, at length retired, but not to sleep. He was *too* much wrought upon by what he had heard to rest quietly, and what snatches of sleep he got, were interrupted by dreams which were anything than pleasant. At eleven o'clock there seemed to be several hundreds of persons crowding into the house. A loud and confused clamour, cursing and cracking of whips, and the noise of chains startled him from his bed; for a moment he would have given the half of his farm in Ohio to have been at home. This uproar was kept up with undulating course, till near morning. There was loud laughing,—loud singing,—loud cursing,—and yet there seemed to be weeping and mourning in the midst of all. Mr. Listwell said he had heard enough during the forepart of the night to convince him that a buyer of men and women stood the best chance of being respected. And he, therefore, thought it best to say nothing which might undo the favorable opinion that had been formed of him in the bar-room by at least one of the fraternity that swarmed about it. While he would not avow himself a purchaser of slaves, he deemed it not prudent to disavow it. He felt that he might, properly, refuse to cast such a pearl before parties which, to him, were worse than swine. To reveal himself, and to impart a knowledge of his real character and sentiments would, to say the least, be imparting intelligence with the certainty of seeing it and himself both abused. Mr. Listwell confesses, that this reasoning did not altogether satisfy his conscience, for, hating slavery as he did, and regarding it to be the immediate duty of every man to cry out against it, "without compromise and without concealment," it was hard for him to admit to himself the possibility of circumstances wherein a man might, properly, hold his tongue on the subject. Having as little of the spirit of a martyr as Erasmus, he concluded, like the latter, that it was wiser to trust the mercy of God for his soul, than the humanity of slave-traders for his body. Bodily fear, not conscientious scruples, prevailed.

In this spirit he rose early in the morning, manifesting no surprise at what he had heard during the night. His quondam friend was soon at his elbow, boring him with all sorts of questions. All, however, directed to find out his character, business, residence, purposes, and destination. With the most perfect appearance of good nature and carelessness, Mr. Listwell evaded these meddlesome inquiries, and turned conversation to general topics, leaving himself and all that specially pertained to him, out of discussion. Disengaging himself from their troublesome companionship, he made his way towards an old bowling-alley, which was connected with the house, and which, like all the rest, was in very bad repair.

On reaching the alley Mr. Listwell saw, for the first time in his life, a slave-gang on their way to market. A sad sight truly. Here were one hundred and thirty human beings,— children of a common Creator—guilty of no crime—men and women, with hearts, minds, and deathless spirits, chained and fettered, and bound for the market, in a christian country,— in a country boasting of its liberty, independence, and high civilization! Humanity converted into merchandise, and linked in iron bands, with no regard to decency or humanity! All sizes, ages, and sexes, mothers, fathers, daughters, brothers, sisters,—all huddled together, on their way to market to be sold and separated from home, and from each other *forever.* And all to fill the pockets of men too lazy to work for an honest living, and who gain their fortune by plundering the helpless, and trafficking in the souls and sinews of men. As he gazed upon this revolting and heart-rending scene, our informant said he almost doubted the existence of a God of justice! And he stood wondering that the earth did not open and swallow up such wickedness.

In the midst of these reflections, and while running his eye up and down the fettered ranks, he met the glance of one whose face he thought he had seen before. To be resolved, he moved towards the spot. It was MADISON WASHINGTON! Here was a scene for the pencil! Had Mr. Listwell been confronted by one risen from the dead, he could not have been more appalled. He was completely stunned. A thunderbolt could not have struck him more dumb. He stood, for a few moments, as motionless as one petrified; collecting himself, he at length exclaimed, *"Madison! is that you?"*

The noble fugitive, but little less astonished than himself, answered cheerily, "O yes, sir, they've got me again."

Thoughtless of consequences for the moment, Mr. Listwell ran up to his old friend, placing his hands upon his shoulders, and looked him in the face! Speechless they stood gazing at each other as if to be doubly resolved that there was no mistake about the matter, till Madison motioned his friend away, intimating a fear lest the keepers should find him there, and suspect him of tampering with the slaves.

"They will soon be out to look after us. You can come when they go to breakfast, and I will tell you all."

Pleased with this arrangement, Mr. Listwell passed out of the alley; but only just in time to save himself, for, while near the door, he observed three men making their way to the alley. The thought occurred to him to await their arrival, as the best means of diverting the ever ready suspicions of the guilty.

While the scene between Mr. Listwell and his friend was going on, the other slaves stood as mute spectators,—at a loss to know what all this could mean. As he left, he heard the man chained to Madison ask, "Who is that gentlemen?"

"He is a friend of mine. I cannot tell you now. Suffice it to say he is a friend. You shall hear more of him before long, but mark me! whatever shall pass between that gentleman and me, in your hearing, I pray you will say nothing about it. We are all chained here together,—ours is a common lot; and that gentleman is not less *your* friend than *mine*." At these words, all mysterious as they were, the unhappy company gave signs of satisfaction and hope. It seems that Madison, by that mesmeric power which is the invariable accompaniment of genius, had already won the confidence of the gang, and was a sort of general-in-chief among them.

By this time the keepers arrived. A horrid trio, well fitted for their demoniacal work. Their uncombed hair came down over foreheads *"villainously low,"* and with eyes, mouths, and noses to match. "Hallo! hallo!" they growled out as they entered. "Are you all there!"

"All here," said Madison.

"Well, well, that's right! your journey will soon be over. You'll be in Richmond by eleven to-day, and then you'll have an easy time on it."

"I say, gal, what in the devil are you crying about?" said one of them. "I'll give you something to cry about, if you don't mind." This was said to a girl, apparently not more than twelve years old, who had been weeping bitterly. She had, probably, left behind her a loving mother, affectionate sisters, brothers, and friends, and her tears were but the natural expression of her sorrow, and the only solace. But the dealers in human flesh have *no* respect for such sorrow. They look upon it as a protest against their cruel injustice, and they are prompt to punish it.

This is a puzzle not easily solved. *How* came he here? what can I do for him? may I not even now be in some way compromised in this affair? were thoughts that troubled Mr. Listwell, and made him eager for the promised opportunity of speaking to Madison.

The bell now sounded for breakfast, and keepers and drivers, with pistols and bowie-knives gleaming from their belts, hurried in, as if to get the best places. Taking the chance now afforded, Mr. Listwell hastened back to the bowling-alley. Reaching Madison, he said, "Now *do* tell me all about the matter. Do you know me?"

"Oh, yes," said Madison, "I know you well, and shall never forget you nor that cold and dreary night you gave me shelter. I must be short," he continued, "for they'll soon be out again. This, then, is the story in brief. On reaching Canada, and getting over the excitement of making my escape, sir, my thoughts turned to my poor wife, who had well deserved my love by her virtuous fidelity and undying affection for me. I could not bear the thought of leaving her in the cruel jaws of slavery, without making an effort to rescue her. First, I tried to get money to buy her; but oh! the process was *too slow*. I despaired of accomplishing it. She was in all my thoughts by day and my dreams by night. At times I could almost hear voice, saying, 'O Madison! Madison! will you then leave me here? can you leave me here to die? No! no! you will come! you will come!' I was wretched. I lost my appetite. I could neither work, eat, nor sleep, till I resolved to hazard my own liberty, to gain that of my wife! But I must be short. Six weeks ago I reached my old master's place. I laid about the neighborhood nearly a week, watching my chance, and, finally, I ventured upon the desperate attempt to reach my poor wife's room by means of a ladder. I reached the window, but the noise in raising it frightened my wife, and she screamed and fainted. I took her in my arms, and was descending the ladder, when the dogs began to bark furiously, and before I could get to the woods the white folks were roused. The cool night air soon restored my wife, and she readily recognized me. We made the best of our way to the woods, but it was now *too* late—the dogs were after us as though they would have torn us to pieces. It was all over with me now! My old master and his two sons ran out with loaded rifles, and before we were out of gunshot, our ears were assailed with *'Stop! stop! or be shot down.'* Nevertheless we ran on. Seeing that we gave no heed to their calls, they fired, and my poor wife fell by my side dead, while I received but a slight flesh wound. I now became desperate, and stood my ground, and awaited their attack over her dead body. They rushed upon me, with their rifles in hand. I parried their blows, and fought them 'till I was knocked down and over-powered."

"Oh! it was madness to have returned," said Mr. Listwell.

"Sir, I could not be free with the galling thought that my poor wife was still a slave. With her in slavery, my body, not my spirit, was free. I was taken to the house,—chained to a ring-bolt,—my wounds dressed. I was kept there three days. All the slaves for miles around, were brought to see me. Many slave-holders came with their slaves, using me as proof of the completeness of their power, and of the impossibility of slaves getting away. I was taunted, jeered at, and berated by them, in a manner that pierced me to the soul. Thank God, I was able to smother my rage, and to bear it all with seeming composure. After my wounds were nearly healed, I was taken to a tree and stripped, and I received sixty lashes on my naked back. A few days after, I was sold to a slave-trader, and placed in this gang for the New Orleans market."

"Do you think your master would sell you to me?"

"O no, sir! I was sold on condition of my being taken South. Their motive is revenge."

"Then, then," said Mr. Listwell, "I fear I can do nothing for you. Put your trust in God, and bear your sad lot with the manly fortitude which becomes a man. I shall see you at Richmond, but don't recognize me." Saying this, Mr. Listwell handed Madison ten dollars; said a few words to the other slaves; received their hearty "God bless you," and made his way to the house.

Fearful of exciting suspicion by too long delay, our friend went to the breakfast table, with the air of one who half reproved the greediness of those who rushed in at the sound of the bell. A cup of coffee was all that he could manage. His feelings were too bitter and excited, and his heart was too full with the fate of poor Madison (whom he loved as well as admired) to relish his breakfast; and although he sat long after the company had left the table, he really did little more than change the position of his knife and fork. The strangeness of meeting again one whom he had met on two several occasions before, under extraordinary circumstances, was well calculated to suggest the idea that a supernatural power, a wakeful providence, or an inexorable fate, had linked their destiny together and that no efforts of his could disentangle him from the mysterious web of circumstances which enfolded him.

On leaving the table, Mr. Listwell nerved himself up and walked firmly into the bar-room. He was at once greeted again by the talkative chatter-box, Mr. Wilkes.

"Them's a likely set of niggers in the alley there," said Wilkes.

"Yes, they're fine looking fellows, one of them I should like to purchase, and for him I would be willing to give a handsome sum."

Turning to one of his comrades, and with a grin of victory, Wilkes said, "Aha, Bill, did you hear that? I told you I know'd that gentleman wanted to buy niggers, and would bid as high as any purchaser in the market."

"Come, come," said Listwell, "don't be too loud in your praise, you are old enough to know that prices rise when purchasers are plenty."

"That's a fact," said Wilkes, "I see you knows the ropes— and there's not a man in old Virginy whom I'd rather help to make a good bargain than you, sir."

Mr. Listwell here threw a dollar at Wilkes, (which the latter caught with a dexterous hand,) saying, "Take that for your kind good will." Wilkes held up the dollar to his right eye, with a grin of victory, and turned to the morose grumbler in the corner who had questioned the liberality of a man of whom he knew nothing.

Mr. Listwell now stood as well with the company as any other occupant of the bar-room.

We pass over the hurry and bustle, the brutal vociferations of the slave-drivers in getting their unhappy gang in motion for Richmond; and we need not narrate every application of the lash to those who faltered in the journey. Mr. Listwell followed the train at a long distance, with a sad heart; and on reaching Richmond, left his horse at a hotel, and made his way to the wharf in the direction of which he saw the slave-coffle driven. He was just in time to see the whole company embark for New Orleans. The thought struck him that, while mixing with the multitude, he might do his friend Madison one last service, and he stept into a hardware store and purchased three strong *files*. These he took with him, and standing near the small boat, which lay in waiting to bear the company by parcels to the side of the brig that lay in the stream, he managed, as Madison passed him, to slip the files into his pocket, and at once darted back among the crowd.

All the company now on board, the imperious voice of the captain sounded, and instantly a dozen hardy seamen were in the rigging, hurrying aloft to unfurl the broad canvas of our Baltimore built American Slaver. The sailors hung about the ropes, like so many black cats, now in the round-tops, now in

20 Many ingenious ways of escape were employed by runaways and the Underground Railroad, including hiding in ships going from Southern to Northern ports. Here we see the smuggling of runaways into Boston at night during the fugitive slave law days

the cross-trees, now on the yard-arms; all was bluster and activity. Soon the broad fore topsail, the royal and top gallant sail were spread to the breeze. Round went the heavy windlass, clank, clank went the fall-bit,—the anchors weighed,—jibs, mainsails, and topsails hauled to the wind, and the long, low, black slaver, with her cargo of human flesh, careened and moved forward to the sea.

Mr. Listwell stood on the shore, and watched the slaver till the last speck of her upper sails faded from sight, and announced the limit of human vision. "Farewell! farewell! brave and true man! God grant that brighter skies may smile upon your future than have yet looked down upon your thorny pathway."

Saying this to himself, our friend lost no time in completing his business, and in making his way homewards, gladly shaking off from his feet the dust of Old Virginia.

Part IV

Oh, where's the slave so lowly
Condemn'd to chains unholy,
    Who could he burst
    His bonds at first
Would pine beneath them slowly?
                    Moore.

————Know ye not
Who would be free, *themselves* must strike the blow.
                    Childe Harold.

What a world of inconsistency, as well as of wickedness, is suggested by the smooth and gliding phrase, AMERICAN SLAVE TRADE; and how strange and perverse is that moral sentiment which loathes, execrates, and brands as piracy and as deserving of death the carrying away into captivity men, women, and children from the *African coast,* but which is neither shocked nor·disturbed by a similar traffic, carried on with the same motives and purposes, and characterized by even more odious peculiarities on the coast of our MODEL REPUBLIC. We execrate and hang the wretch guilty of this crime on the coast of Guinea, while we respect and applaud the guilty participators in this murderous business on the enlightened shores of the Chesapeake. The inconsistency is so flagrant and glaring, that it would seem to cast a doubt on the doctrine of the innate moral sense of mankind.

Just two months after the sailing of the Virginia slave brig, which the reader has seen move off to sea so proudly with her human cargo for the New Orleans market, there chanced to meet, in the Marine Coffee-house at Richmond, a company of *ocean birds,* when the following conversation, which throws some light on the subsequent history, not only of Madison Washington, but of the hundred and thirty human beings with whom we last saw him chained.

"I say, shipmate, you had rather rough weather on your late passage to Orleans?" said Jack Williams, a regular old salt, tauntingly, to a trim, compact, manly looking person, who proved to be the first mate of the slave brig in question.

"Foul play, as well as foul weather," replied the firmly knit personage, evidently but little inclined to enter upon a subject which terminated so ingloriously to the captain and officers of the American slaver.

"Well, betwixt you and me," said Williams, "that whole affair on board of the Creole was miserably and disgracefully managed. Those black rascals got the upper hand of ye altogether; and, in my opinion, the whole disaster was the result of ignorance of the real character of *darkies* in general. With half a dozen *resolute* white men, (I say it not boastingly,) I could have had the rascals in irons in ten minutes, not because I'm so strong, but I know how to manage 'em. With my back against the *caboose,* I could, myself, have flogged a dozen of them; and had I been on board, by every monster of the deep, every black devil of 'em all would have had his neck stretched from the yard-arm. Ye made a mistake in yer manner of fighting 'em. All that is needed in dealing with a set of rebellious *darkies,* is to show that yer not afraid of 'em. For my own part, I would not honor a dozen niggers by pointing a gun at one on 'em,—a good stout whip, or a stiff rope's end, is better than all the guns at Old Point to quell a *nigger* insurrection. Why, sir, to take a gun to a *nigger* is the best way you can select to tell him you are afraid of him, and the best way of inviting his attack."

This speech made quite a sensation among the company, and a part of them indicated solicitude for the answer which might be made to it. Our first mate replied, "Mr. Williams, all that you've now said sounds very well *here* on shore, where, perhaps, you have studied negro character. I do not profess to understand the subject as well as yourself; but it strikes me, you apply the same rule in dissimilar cases. It is quite easy to talk of flogging niggers here on land, where you have the sympathy of the community, and the whole physical force of the government, State and national, at your command; and where, if a negro shall lift his hand against a white man, the whole community, with one accord, are ready to unite in shooting him down. I say, in such circumstances, it's easy to talk of flogging negroes and of negro cowardice; but, sir, I deny that the negro is, naturally, a coward, or that your theory of managing slaves will stand the test of *salt* water. It may do very well for an overseer, a contemptible hireling, to take advantage of fears already in existence, and which his presence has no power to inspire; to swagger about whip in hand, and discourse on the timidity and cowardice of negroes; for they have a smooth sea and a fair wind. It is one thing to manage a company of slaves on a Virginia plantation, and quite another thing to quell an insurrection on the lonely billows of the Atlantic, where every breeze speaks of courage and liberty. For the negro to act cowardly on shore, may be to act wisely; and I've some doubts whether *you*, Mr. Williams, would find it very convenient were you a slave in Algiers, to raise your hand against the bayonets of a whole government."

"By George, shipmate," said Williams, "you're coming rather *too* near. Either I've fallen very low in your estimation, or your notions of negro courage have got up a button-hole too high. Now I more than ever wish I'd been on board of that luckless craft. I'd have given ye practical evidence of the truth of my theory. I don't doubt there's some difference in being at sea. But a nigger's a nigger, on sea or land; and is a coward, find him where you will; a drop of blood from one on 'em will skeer a hundred. A knock on the nose, or a kick on the shin, will tame the wildest *'darkey'* you can fetch me. I say again, and will stand by it, I could, with half a dozen good men, put the whole nineteen on 'em in irons, and have carried them safe to New Orleans too. Mind, I don't blame you, but I do say, and every gentleman here will bear me out in it, that the fault was somewhere, or them niggers would never have got off as they have done. For my part I feel ashamed to have the idea go abroad, that a ship load of slaves can't be safely taken from Richmond to New Orleans. I should like, merely to redeem the character of Virginia sailors, to take charge of a ship load on 'em to-morrow."

Williams went on in this strain, occasionally casting an imploring glance at the company for applause for his wit, and sympathy for his contempt of negro courage. He had, evidently, however, waked up the wrong passenger; for besides being in the right, his opponent carried that in his eye which marked him a man not to be trifled with.

"Well, sir," said the sturdy mate, "you can select your own method for distinguishing yourself;—the path of ambition in this direction is quite open to you in Virginia, and I've no doubt that you will be highly appreciated and compensated for all your valiant achievements in that line; but for myself, while I do not profess to be a giant, I have resolved never to set my foot on the deck of a slave ship, either as officer, or common sailor again; I have got enough of it."

"Indeed! indeed!" exclaimed Williams, derisively.

"Yes, *indeed,*" echoed the mate; "but don't misunderstand me. It is not the high value that I set upon my life that makes me say what I have said; yet I'm resolved never to endanger my life again in a cause which my conscience does not approve. I dare say *here* what many men *feel,* but *dare not speak,* that this whole slave-trading business is a disgrace and scandal to Old Virginia."

"Hold! hold on! shipmate," said Williams, "I hardly thought you'd have shown your colors so soon,—I'll be hanged if you're not as good an abolitionist as Garrison himself."

The mate now rose from his chair, manifesting some excitement. "What do you mean, sir," said he, in a commanding tone. *"That man does not live who shall offer me an insult with impunity."*

The effect of these words was marked; and the company clustered around. Williams, in an apologetic tone, said, "Shipmate! keep your temper. I meant no insult. We all know that Tom Grant is no coward, and what I said about your being an abolitionist was simply this: you *might* have put down them black mutineers and murderers, but your conscience held you back."

"In that, too," said Grant, "you were mistaken. I did all that any man with equal strength and presence of mind could have done. The fact is, Mr. Williams, you underrate the courage as well as the skill of these negroes, and further, you do not seem to have been correctly informed about the case in hand at all."

"All I know about it is," said Williams, "that on the ninth day after you left Richmond, a dozen or two of the niggers ye had on board, came on deck and took the ship from you;— had her steered into a British port, where, by the by, every woolly head of them went ashore and was free. Now I take this to be a discreditable piece of business, and one demanding explanation."

"There are a great many discreditable things in the world," said Grant. "For a ship to go down under a calm sky is, upon the first flush of it, disgraceful either to sailors or caulkers. But when we learn, that by some mysterious disturbance in nature, the waters parted beneath, and swallowed the ship up, we lose our indignation and disgust in lamentation of the disaster, and in awe of the Power which controls the elements."

"Very true, very true," said Williams, "I should be very glad to have an explanation which would relieve the affair of its present discreditable features. I have desired to see you ever since you got home, and to learn from you a full statement of the facts in the case. To me the whole thing seems unaccountable. I cannot see how a dozen or two of ignorant negroes, not one of whom had ever been to sea before, and all of them were closely ironed between decks, should be able to get their fetters off, rush out of the hatchway in open daylight, kill two white men, the one the captain and the other their master, and then carry the ship into a British port, where every 'darkey' of them was set free. There must have been great carelessness, or cowardice somewhere!"

The company which had listened in silence during most of this discussion, now became much excited. One said, "I agree with Williams"; and several said "the thing looks black enough." After the temporary tumultuous exclamations had subsided,—

"I see," said Grant, "how you regard this case, and how difficult it will be for me to render our ship's company blameless in your eyes. Nevertheless, I will state the fact precisely as they came under my own observation. Mr. Williams speaks of 'ignorant negroes,' and, as a general rule, they are ignorant; but had he been on board the *Creole* as I was, he would have seen cause to admit that there are exceptions to this general rule. The leader of the mutiny in question was just as shrewd a fellow as ever I met in my life, and was as well fitted to lead in a dangerous enterprise as any one white man in ten thousand. The name of this man, strange to say, (ominous of greatness,) was MADISON WASHINGTON. In the short time he had been on board, he had secured the confidence of every officer. The negroes fairly worshipped him. His manner and bearing were such, that no one could suspect him of a murderous purpose. The only feeling with which we regarded him was, that he was a powerful, good-disposed negro. He seldom spoke to any one, and when he did speak, it was with the utmost propriety. His words were well chosen, and his pronunciation equal to that of any schoolmaster. It was a mystery to us *where* he got his knowledge of language; but as little was said to him, none of us knew the extent of his intelligence and ability till it was too late. It seems he brought three files with him on board, and must have gone to work upon his fetters the first night out; and he must have worked well at that; for on the day of the rising, he got the irons *off eighteen* besides himself.

"The attack began just about twilight in the evening. Apprehending a squall, I had commanded the second mate to order all hands on deck, to take in sail. A few minutes before this I had seen Madison's head above the hatchway, looking out upon the white-capped waves at the leeward. I think I never saw him look more good-natured. I stood just about midship, on the larboard side. The captain was pacing the quarter-deck on the starboard side, in company with Mr. Jameson, the owner of most of the slaves on board. Both were armed. I had just told the men to lay aloft, and was looking to see my orders obeyed, when I heard the discharge of a pistol on the starboard side; and turning suddenly around, the very deck seemed covered with fiends from the pit. The nineteen negroes were all on deck, with their broken fetters in their hands, rushing in all directions. I put my hand quickly in my pocket to draw out my jack-knife; but before I could draw it, I was knocked senseless to the deck. When I came to myself, (which I did in a few minutes, I suppose, for it was yet quite light,) there was not a white man on deck. The sailors were all aloft in the rigging, and dared not come down. Captain Clarke and Mr. Jameson lay stretched on the quarter-deck,—both dying,—while Madison himself stood at the helm unhurt.

"I was completely weakened by the loss of blood, and had not recovered from the stunning blow which felled me to the deck; but it was a little too much for me, even in my prostrate condition, to see our good brig commanded by a *black murderer.* So I called out to the men to come down and take the ship, or die in the attempt. Suiting the action to the word, I started aft. 'You murderous villain,' said I, to the imp at the helm, and rushed upon him to deal him a blow, when he pushed me back with his strong, black arm, as though I had been a boy of twelve. I looked around for the men. They were still in the rigging. Not one had come down. I started towards Madison again. The rascal now told me to stand back. 'Sir,' said he, 'your life is in my hands. I could have killed you a dozen times over during this last half hour, and could kill you now. You call me a *black murderer.* I am not a murderer. God is my witness that LIBERTY, not *malice,* is the motive for this night's work. I have done no more to those dead men yonder, than they would have done to me in like circumstances. We have struck for our freedom, and if a true man's heart be in you, you will honor us for the deed. We have done that which you applaud your fathers for doing, and if we are murderers, *so were they!*'

"I felt little disposition to reply to this impudent speech. By heaven, it disarmed me. The fellow loomed up before me. I forgot his blackness in the dignity of his manner, and the eloquence of his speech. It seemed as if the souls of both the great dead (whose names he bore) had entered him. To the sailors in the rigging he said: 'Men! the battle is over,—your captain is dead. I have complete command of this vessel. All resistance to my authority will be in vain. My men have won their liberty, with no other weapons but their own BROKEN FETTERS. We are nineteen in number. We do not thirst for your blood, we demand only our rightful freedom. Do not flatter yourselves that I am ignorant of chart or compass. I know both. We are now only about sixty miles from Nassau. Come down, and do your duty. Land us in Nassau, and not a hair of your heads shall be hurt.'

"I shouted, *Stay where you are, men,*—when a sturdy black fellow ran at me with a handspike, and would have split my head open, but for the interference of Madison, who darted between me and the blow. 'I know what you are up to,' said the latter to me. 'You want to navigate this brig into a slave port, where you would have us all hanged; but you'll miss it; before this brig shall touch a slave-cursed shore while I am on board, I will myself put a match to the magazine, and blow her, and be blown with her, into a thousand fragments. Now I have saved your life twice within the last twenty minutes, —for, when you lay helpless on deck, my men were about to kill you. I held them in check. And if you now (seeing I am your friend and not your enemy) persist in your resistance to my authority, I give you fair warning, YOU SHALL DIE.'

"Saying this to me, he cast a glance into the rigging where the terror-stricken sailors were clinging, like so many frightened monkeys, and commanded them to come down, in a tone from which there was no appeal; for four men stood by with muskets in hand, ready at the word of command to shoot them down.

"I now became satisfied that resistance was out of the question; that my best policy was to put the brig into Nassau, and secure the assistance of the American consul at that port. I felt sure that the authorities would enable us to secure the murderers, and bring them to trial.

"By this time the apprehended squall had burst upon us. The wind howled furiously—the ocean was white with foam, which, on account of the darkness, we could see only by the quick flashes of lightning that darted occasionally from the angry sky. All was alarm and confusion. Hideous cries came up from the slave women. Above the roaring billows a succession of heavy thunder rolled along, swelling the terrific din. Owing to the great darkness, and a sudden shift of the wind, we found ourselves in the trough of the sea. When shipping a heavy sea over the starboard bow, the bodies of the captain and Mr. Jameson were washed overboard. For awhile we had dearer interests to look after than slave property. A more savage thunder-gust never swept the ocean. Our brig rolled and creaked as if every bolt would be started, and every thread of oakum would be pressed out of the seams. 'To the pumps! to the pumps!' I cried, but not a sailor would quit his grasp. Fortunately this squall soon passed over, or we must have been food for sharks.

"During all the storm, Madison stood firmly at the helm, —his keen eye fixed upon the binnacle. He was not indifferent to the dreadful hurricane; yet he met it with the equanimity of an old sailor. He was silent but not agitated. The first words he uttered after the storm had slightly subsided, were characteristic of the man. 'Mr. mate, you cannot write the bloody laws of slavery on those restless billows. The ocean, if not the land, is free.' I confess, gentlemen, I felt myself in the presence of a superior man; one who, had he been a white man, I would have followed willingly and gladly in any honorable enterprise. Our difference of color was the only ground for difference of action. It was not that his principles were wrong in the abstract; for they are the principles of 1776. But I could not bring myself to recognize their application to one whom I deemed my inferior.

"But to my story. What happened now is soon told. Two hours after the frightful tempest had spent itself, we were plump at the wharf in Nassau. I sent two of our men immediately to our consul with a statement of facts, requesting his interference in our behalf. What he did, or whether he did anything, I don't know; but, by order of the authorities, a company of *black* soldiers came on board, for the purpose, as they said, of protecting the property. These impudent rascals, when I called on them to assist me in keeping the slaves on board, sheltered themselves adroitly under their instructions only to protect property,—and said they did not recognize *persons* as *property.* I told them that by the laws of Virginia and the laws of the United States, the slaves on board were as much property as the barrels of flour in the hold. At this the stupid blockheads showed their *ivory,* rolled up their white eyes in horror, as if the idea of putting men on a footing with merchandise were revolting to their humanity. When these instructions were understood among the negroes, it was impossible for us to keep them on board. They deliberately gathered up their baggage before our eyes, and, against our remonstrances, poured through the gangway,—formed themselves into a procession on the wharf,—bid farewell to all on board, and, uttering the wildest shouts of exultation, they marched, amidst the deafening cheers of a multitude of sympathizing spectators, under the triumphant leadership of their heroic chief and deliverer, MADISON WASHINGTON."

SUGGESTIONS FOR FURTHER READING

With the exception of *The Heroic Slave* by Frederick Douglass and the petition by Belinda, all the narratives in this book are extracts from larger works. Most of the original sources of these are rare and out of print, though some American libraries have copies in their collections. Recently, however, quite a few slave narratives have been reprinted, and there are many slave narratives and stories by Black writers that illuminate slavery and slave life besides those included in this book. Some additional books of interest are:

Black Thunder by Arna Bontemps. Published in England by Seven Seas Books. A historical novel by a leading twentieth-century Black writer, that dramatizes the true story of a slave revolt—Gabriel's Revolt in Virginia in 1800.

Jubilee by Margaret Walker. Published in England by Hodder and Stoughton. A historical novel, again by a leading Black writer, that presents the fullest and most vivid picture of slavery, as the slaves felt and experienced it, in American fiction.

Lay My Burden Down: A Folk History of Slavery edited by B. A. Botkin and published by the University of Chicago Press. A selection of extracts from the Slave Narrative Collection of the Federal Writer's Project, consisting of interviews with surviving former slaves conducted between 1936 and 1938.

My Bondage and My Freedom by Frederick Douglass. Black Rediscovery Series, published by Dover Publications. A classic of slave narrative literature, originally published in 1855.

Narrative of the Life of Frederick Douglass, an American Slave, Written by Himself. A classic by the most famous of the runaways, originally published in 1845, reprinted in paperback by New American Library.

The Narrative of William W. Brown, a Fugitive Slave. Published by Addison-Wesley. A paperback reprint of this important slave narrative originally published in 1848.

Printed in Great Britain by Photolitho-offset
by Cox & Wyman Limited · London · Fakenham · Reading